LAND OF A MILLION ELEPHANTS

Memoirs
C^{OF A} *anadian* *Peacekeeper*

by
Lt. Colonel John E.G. de Domenico

Published by

GENERAL STORE
PUBLISHING HOUSE

1 Main Street, Burnstown, Ontario, Canada K0J 1G0
Telephone 1-800-465-6072 Fax 613-432-7184

ISBN 1-896182-80-1
Printed and bound in Canada
Layout and Design by Derek McEwen

Copyright © John E.G. de Domenico

Canadian Cataloguing in Publication Data
    Land of a million elephants : memoirs of a Canadian peacekeeper

ISBN 1-896182-80-1

    1. de Domenico, John E. G., 1925
    2. United Nations–Armed Forces–Canada–Biography.
    3. Canada. Canadian Army. Royal Canadian Artillery.
        –Biography. I. Title.

FC3076.1.D43A3 1997   355.3'57'092   C97-901209-0
F1058.D43 1997

Index

To my wife, my sons and their families

Peace, it has been said, is the most precious commodity
the world has to offer. I therefore also dedicate this work
to the politicians who authorise peace keeping activities, to
the generals who plan them but, most of all to the ordinary
servicemen who put it all together in the face of many
adversities.

John de Domenico

Land of a Million Elephants

Sources

THIS BOOK is primarily based on my personal reminiscences aided by those of my colleagues who volunteered their assistance.

The following material has been consulted:

- An Interim Report on the Activities of the International Commission for Supervision and Control in Laos from the Date of its Establishment to 31st December 1954—Public Archives Canada and National Library of Canada.

- Maps courtesy of Document Exchange NIA, United States Department of State.

- Compton's Interactive Encyclopedia, 1997 Edition.

Foreword

by

Major General A. James Tedlie, D.S.O, K.St.J., C.D., M.A.

READING JOHN DE DOMENICO'S compelling account of his experiences as a member of the International Commission for Supervision and Control in Indo China brought back a flood of memories both sacred and profane.

As one who was a member of this group of Canadians, I believe that de Domenico has caught the rich flavour of service in a completely foreign, and to us little known, part of the world.

It is particularly interesting when de Domenico recalls that while Canada made her usual speedy response by offering to help at a time of international crisis, our relevant expertise was of a very low order. This was another case of the always willing, never ready attitude that has plagued Canada's peace-keeping efforts to this very day

Any success that we have achieved in these international endeavours is due to the adaptability and the devotion to duty of Canadians such as de Domenico. Through the descriptions of day to day activities and less than comfortable conditions, the reader is given a true glimpse of the dedication and fortitude displayed by our fellow citizens when representing their country in foreign lands.

The author's light hearted description of air travel to and from the Orient in a noisy RCAF North Star aircraft and of travelling in the rather dilapidated flying machines operated by the local airlines in Indo China are examples of the less than comfortable conditions experienced by those who served on the Commission.

The interaction between Canadian and Polish members of the Commission is well documented by de Domenico. Their widely divergent political philosophies made it inevitable that there would be conflicting opinions during many of the investigations. It is a matter of record that de Domenico and his colleagues were never swayed by communistic ideological rhetoric. They maintained a neutral position in investigating the many clashes between the warring factions.

The author's account of the contrast between life in Hanoi under French rule and life after the Communist take over by the forces of Ho Chi Minh is a sterling example of what takes place when a colonial power is replaced by a well-led populist movement. Living in Hanoi during this period was an unforgettable experience.

I highly recommend de Domenico's interesting book to all those who wish to learn about what goes on at the grassroots when Canadians go to help keep the peace. Even those not specifically interested in this very topical subject will find it to be a great read.

A. James Tedlie

Sidney, British Columbia
23 February 1997.

Prologue

CONSIDER THE ELEPHANT. It is large and provides a high perch from which the rider can maintain a lookout for any dangers lurking ahead. It has high mobility and can manoeuvre through thick jungle unafraid of any other wild animals. As Hannibal demonstrated, it can even traverse mountainous terrain. This huge animal is incredibly strong and can be trained to use its trunk to manipulate with amazing dexterity heavy objects like felled trees and to carry heavy loads. The elephant eats a great deal but it can forage for itself quite nicely. It does not require a maintenance organisation to keep it in running order. In short, in a hot country where labour is very hard and where technology is in its infancy, the elephant is a truly invaluable property.

Consider now a million elephants. In an era when people had not become accustomed—as we have become—to speaking in billions or trillions, a million elephants was truly a measure of enormous riches. In much the same way as North Americans extol the many virtues of their land in terms of natural resources, Laotians describe their country as "The Land of a Million Elephants."

Hence the title of this autobiographical account of a young Canadian's experiences in Indochina—mostly Laos—in the earliest days (1954-55) of the International Commission for Supervision and Control (ICSC) in Indochina. It focuses on the role played by Canada in one of its earliest peace-keeping involvements as a member of the ICSC in Viet Nam, Cambodia and Laos. In the light of the tragedy that was later to befall this troubled area, it is perhaps difficult to see where we, the pioneers of the ICSC, made any dent on the history of these unfortunate countries. And yet, for a number of years, the ICSC was instrumental in preserving a modicum of peace to help the people of Indochina through a difficult period of transition from French colonial rule to independence. I believe this to be one of Canada's significant contributions to the peace of the world.

From a personal standpoint, I derive satisfaction from knowing that some families—albeit too few—were reunited as a result of our efforts to track the young men who had been "forcibly recruited" (kidnapped) by the retreating communist forces. We probably saved some lives when we were able to place ourselves in harm's way when skirmishes broke out between the former enemies. Most of all we demonstrated to the Indochinese people that somebody on the other side of the world cared enough to make the effort for it was not without its personal and national sacrifices. On the other side of the ledger, service with the ICSC was a stimulating and adventurous experience for most of us.

I am prompted to share this experience with the reader because I feel a desire to place on record an account of an event in Canada's history which is fast being forgotten. I make no pretences: this book is not a profound study. It is merely a collection of light-hearted reminiscences from which the reader will hopefully derive some enjoyment. The reader may also gain a better understanding of the intricacies of peace-keeping. The tales I tell are primarily drawn from my own recollections. My memory however has been sharpened by the recollections, letters and photographs which have been generously showered upon me by a number of my colleagues who shared centre stage with me in Indochina and who were kind enough to offer me some much-needed moral support during the preparation of this book. There were many times when the blank sheet of paper in my typewriter proved almost too daunting. The generous support of my colleagues was often the only thing that stood between me and the waste-paper basket. I am particularly mindful of the debt of gratitude I owe to Major Gilles Perodeau of the Canadian Guards, Major Pete Petrick of the Royal Canadian Corps of Signals and to Major Percy Davis of the Royal Canadian

Artillery. There were many others. Though their names escape me now, I remember them as accounts payable in my life's ledger.

Most importantly, I pay tribute at the outset to my wife Madge who managed her pregnancy and the household so capably in my absence. In such situations, the contributions made by the stay-at-homes are often forgotten. Well, Madge, yours isn't!

John de Domenico

Southeast Asia

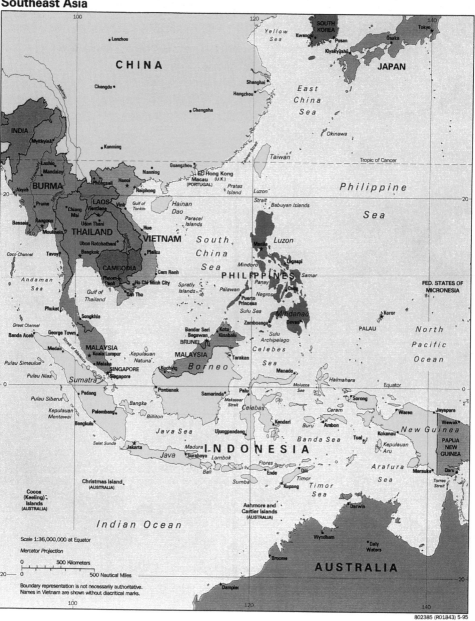

Scale 1:36,000,000 at Equator

Mercator Projection

0   500 Kilometers
0   500 Nautical Miles

Boundary representation is not necessarily authoritative.
Names in Vietnam are shown without diacritical marks.

802385 (R01843) 5-95

Introduction

FRANCE HAD LINKS with Viet Nam since the early seventeenth century through the establishment of a successful Jesuit mission in Danang. In the 1880s, France occupied Indochina to help strengthen herself politically and economically by establishing an empire. Viet Nam supplied the West with tin, rubber and rice.

After the defeat in Europe of the French in 1940, France was forced to grant the Japanese the right to station troops and aircraft in Indochina. On 9 March 1945, the Japanese deposed the French administration and took over control of the region. This however was short-lived. In August 1945, the Japanese empire collapsed and the Japanese were forced to evacuate Indochina. Under the terms of the Potsdam agreement, two zones of occupation were established in Indochina until the French could reoccupy their former colony. Chinese Nationalist forces occupied the area of Viet Nam North of the 17th parallel while British troops occupied the South. Soon after, the Chinese troops in the "Ky" of Tonkin were withdrawn creating a vacuum. Ho Chi Minh (One Who Enlightens), the leader of the Viet Minh (short for Viet Nam Doc Lop Dong Minh) or the National Front for the Independence of Viet Nam quickly filled this void. The independence of North Viet Nam was declared on 2 September 1945 and a provisional government was set up by Ho Chi Minh.

Because there were insufficient French troops to dispute this provisional government, France agreed to a meeting in March 1946 with Ho Chi Minh. At this meeting the parties agreed that the Democratic Republic of Viet Nam would have the status of a free state within the French union. This arrangement was regarded by Ho

Chi Minh as a temporary compromise and fighting soon broke out between the Viet Minh and the French forces.

In November and December of 1953, the French established an entrenched camp in Dien Bien Phu just east of the Laotian-North Viet Nam border on a wide, fertile plain. The town was at the crossroads of several highways connecting the northern part of North Viet Nam and northern Laos. Ten thousand men were deployed partly to protect Laos but mainly to try and draw Viet Minh forces into an open battle at which the French forces could bring their equipment superiority to bear decisively. By 13 March 1954 however, the Viet Minh forces overran two French strong points defending the airstrip which was the supply lifeline of the French garrison. After fifty-five days of fighting, on 7 May 1954, the French garrison, commanded by Brigadier General De Castries, was forced to capitulate.

The battle of Dien Bien Phu—as it was to become known—brought the final curtain down on the drama of the French Indochina War. The French badly underestimated their enemy. The French could not be made to consider even the possibility that a rag-tag army such as the Viet Minh could emerge victorious in a battle fought over open terrain. The Viet Minh, after all, was a guerrilla army trained to fight from the cover of thick jungle. The deck seemed very much stacked against the Viet Minh. Whereas the French had a great deal of air support, the Viet Minh had none. The mountainous terrain surrounding Dien Bien Phu would preclude the transport of weapons and the huge quantities of heavy and bulky artillery ammunition. The French did not count on the determination of the North Vietnamese. Literally thousands of peasants were recruited to form a human chain carrying weapons and supplies on their backs and lashed to bicycles over hundreds of miles. The French did not count either on the generalship of the Commander-in-Chief of the Viet Minh force, General Vo Nguyen Giap, or on the fanaticism of the troops he led.

It was the second debacle suffered by the French in less than two decades. Only this time it was not at the hands of a well-trained, highly disciplined German army supported by hundreds of tanks and Stuka dive-bombers. This time it was at the hands of a guerrilla force recruited from the ranks of peasant farmers.

The French now needed a helping hand to extricate themselves from the situation as honourably as possible. That hand was extended by the British who persuaded the Russians to join them in helping to bring the French Indochina War to an end.

The decision to hold a conference in Geneva to resolve the Indochina situation was made in February 1954. Under the co-chairmanship of the United Kingdom and the Union of Socialist Soviet Republics, the deliberations started on 9 May 1954.

The parties to the conference were France, China, the UK, the USSR, the USA, Laos, Cambodia and the two governments of Viet Nam. Canada kept a watchful brief on the proceedings through normal diplomatic contacts. After several restricted and plenary sessions, the conference ended its deliberations on 21 July 1954 and reached an agreement on the cessation of hostilities in Indochina. This agreement recognised the independence of Laos, Cambodia and Viet Nam. It temporarily placed Viet Nam under two separate administrations using the seventeenth parallel of latitude as the demarcation line. Free elections were to be held in three hundred days to reunite Viet Nam.

Cease-fires were to come into effect by 8am on 11 August 1954. After eight years of war, approximately four hundred thousand dead and three months of negotiation, all of Indochina would now be at peace. French and Viet Minh forces which were on the wrong side of the demarcation line at the time of the cease-fire were to withdraw to their assigned territories. Reinforcements were to be restricted so that the military strength of the respective forces in Indochina would be frozen at the pre-cease-fire levels. With the exception of Laos and Cambodia, foreign military bases were prohibited.

While the belligerents were responsible for the implementation of the terms of the agreement, the Geneva conference established an International Commission for Supervision and Control in Indochina. The ICSC was to have a purely supervisory role and was in no way responsible for the execution of the terms of the agreement. The ICSC was to be a tripartite arrangement with representation from the Western and Eastern blocs and with a non-aligned nation in the chair. Canada, Poland and India filled the respective bill.

Canada did not have any direct interest in Indochina. In fact, its only contact with that part of the world was through a missionary presence. There were however historical , political and humanitarian reasons which prompted Canada to accept as onerous a responsibility as Indochina.

Our close historical ties with France encouraged us to do whatever we could to enable the French to extricate themselves with honour from a situation which had become militarily and politically untenable. The Geneva agreement achieved that but the armistice needed policing by both East and West if it was to be credible. None of the European countries could do much so soon after the Second World War. The United States was obviously unacceptable. Canada seemed to be the best placed among the Western democracies for a task such as Indochina.

The outbreak of hostilities in Korea lent credence to the then-popular theory of a fight against communism in Asia using Viet Nam, Korea and Formosa as the three points of a thrust into the underbelly of Red China and eventually, who knows, the Soviet Union. This theory, coupled with the possibilities of armed intervention in Indochina which existed at that time, made the likelihood of the escalation of the war in Indochina into a global conflict very real. It was in Canada's interest to do what it could to minimise the possibility of such an eventuality.

An involvement in Indochina was also seen as further evidence of Canada's emergence from its colonial past. The Balfour Declaration and the enactment of the Statute of Westminster in 1931 proclaimed Canada's sovereignty in international as well as domestic affairs. This however needed frequent re-enforcement. In 1939, for example, Canada deliberately delayed declaring war on Germany by one week after Great Britain's move in this direction. At the risk of dividing the nation, Canada made a significant contribution to the allied war effort. In spite of this, Canada was not made party to the grand strategy of the allies for global peace after the successful conclusion of the Second World War. A commitment in Indochina further reinforced Canada's standing as a sovereign member of the international community. Finally, the personality and deep personal interest in world peace of its Foreign Minister (Lester B. Pearson) was dominant enough to encourage Canada to participate in this new international venture.

Indochina was to be the first of a string of peacekeeping opportunities for Mr. Pearson to display his abiding interest in the maintenance of world peace. In October 1956, for example, Israel, France and Great Britain invaded the Suez Canal zone in order to ensure free passage of ships through the canal. Led by the United States, the world expressed strong disapproval of this action and the invaders were obliged to call a halt to the operation. A truce was arranged by the United Nations which provided for the deployment of a UN force in the Suez Canal zone. Mr. Pearson played a leading role in these complicated negotiations and offered Canadian participation in the force.

Accordingly, Canada accepted the invitation to participate in the ICSC. It contributed twenty five civilians and one hundred and thirty-five military personnel to the business. Each of the member states established a headquarters of ambassadorial rank in each of the four countries of Indochina. The military components of the three delegations were organised into a number of fixed and mobile teams which were to be deployed to various locations within Indochina with the agreement of the former belligerents. The teams were to have complete freedom of movement and were entrusted with the task of keeping their ambassadors informed of the progress of the execution phase of the armistice. As we shall see, the freedom of movement provision was to become a bone of contention and the final compromise detracted considerably from the credibility of the Commission.

For some time the US had been playing a supporting role to the French in Indochina A great deal of planning had already gone into the provision by the US of combat air and logistic support to the French garrison at Dien Bien Phu. Congress however was fearful that the deployment of US ground forces in Indochina might provoke China into taking a more active part in the fighting and that eventually the commitment of significant US ground forces to the war in Indochina would have become a distinct possibility. In the event, no US support was rendered to the garrison at Dien Bien Phu.

The US was officially a participant in the Geneva conference but it played only a minor role in the deliberations. Its support of the agreement was lukewarm. In a declaration by the US delegation at the end of the conference, the US reiterated its traditional position that peoples are entitled to determine their own future and committed the US not to depart from this position. Effectively, the US disassociated itself from the agreement. It disapproved of parleying with Communist governments and washed its hands of the whole affair. The United States Congress never did ratify the agreement. The Americans proceeded to breathe life into the fledgling South Vietnamese forces in the hope that this would suffice to stop any North Vietnamese incursions into South Viet Nam.

The rest is history. The text of the agreement on the cessation of hostilities in Laos reached by the Geneva Conference may be found at Appendix "A." This introduction is a brief summary and the reader may wish to consult the many books which exist for a more detailed description of the political, economic and military events which transpired prior to the arrival of the ICSC.

Chapter 1

HANOI OR BUST

THE HEAT WAVES SHIMMERED over Quinte Bay making it difficult to see the red sleeve target towed through the sky by an air force plane. Some Militia units were firing their 40mm Bofors in the general direction of the target. To the dismay of the pilot, they occasionally aimed off ahead a little too far and came uncomfortably close to the towing aircraft. Not surprisingly, the pilot used to get quite upset about such things; he and I had many interesting conversations at the bar about this subject. Aside from organising the training in anti-aircraft artillery of the militiamen, I was also required during firing practices to stand on the high safety tower with a whistle in my mouth holding a large red flag. When I saw the fire getting close to the towing aircraft, I would blow the whistle and wave the flag to make the gunners cease firing. It was a hot, boring job and I had a bad head for heights so, any break in the monotony would have been most welcome. It came in the form of a message from our headquarters in Picton, Ontario summoning me to report immediately to the School of Artillery Commandant. Since my conscience was not exactly clear after last night's party at the mess, it was not quite the respite I had hoped for from my duties at the firing camp.

But "theirs is not to reason why" and I was soon saluting the Adjutant who was being at his uncommunicative best. He would not say what the summons was all about and said the Commandant would be a little late and would I please have a seat in the waiting area. There were three other officers waiting and, since none of them had been involved in last night's party, we couldn't make a connection. The mystery about the reason for our summons deepened and the things we did to our fingernails were not very nice.

Alfie Hood was not exactly the most congenial of Commandants. He was a very stern man, a stickler for sobriety and high standards of performance. He had a demeanour which terrified junior officers. He breezed into the Adjutant's office, squeezed his very large frame past the desk and nodded us into his spacious office.

"You young pups are going out to Indochina," he blurted out, fixing each of us in turn with a piercing look from those icy blue eyes of his.

"Indochina?" we muttered almost in unison. I, for one, was only vaguely aware that the French had been battling Ho Chi Minh's people for a number of years but I can't honestly say that the affair held any deep and abiding interest to me.

"Yes, Indochina," the Colonel said "and I don't want any arguments from you." Once more that piercing look. "The Adjutant will brief you on all the details; in the meantime, all four of you are relieved of all duties. Dismissed!"

In something of a daze, we saluted as smartly as we could and marched out of his office. Actually, Alfie was not a bad fellow. I learned later that he did not relish the idea of sending four of his young officers to a remote corner of the world without any special training or psychological preparation. He also did not know very much about the whole thing except that our departure date was just a few days around the corner. He was also aware of the fact that this quick foreign posting would inevitably create some quite serious problems to most of us. I had only just returned from a two-year course in gunnery in Wales and I was not expecting a foreign posting so soon after. More importantly, my wife was six months pregnant and since we had emigrated to Canada only a few years earlier, we had no relatives in Canada on whom we could lean. Indochina was of course an unaccompanied posting; Madge would have to look after things as best as she could. It was rather interesting to read a press release from the Chief of the General Staff a few days later in which he claimed that the officers and men who had been selected were his own personal choices and that one of the factors which he had considered in making the selections was that none of us had any personal problems to contend with!

The Adjutant had very little to add except that we would be leaving Canada in about three weeks and that, after three days' leave, we were to report to an indoctrination area that had been established in Kingston, Ontario.

Madge was calling on the Gowlands who lived in Cherry Valley. We were good friends and we dropped in on each other for tea every now and then. By the time I got to their house, I had become quite excited about the prospect of a year in the Far East. I had never been to that part of the world and the job seemed interesting and challenging. In fact, I had become quite enthusiastic and I almost forgot that the baby's delivery would be in the very near future. Madge was a good soldier and she too got caught up in the excitement. While we had no close relatives to lean on, the army was like a big family and our friends would make sure that all went well. We talked excitedly about the journey out there and the job I would be doing. The latter was a very brief conversation because I had absolutely no idea what the job was all about. We also discussed the various domestic arrangements, such as banking, that we would have to conclude in the next three days.

The short leave passed quickly and I was soon knocking on the doors of the Royal Canadian Electrical and Mechanical Engineers School in Kingston. The Canadian contingent was being assembled there for the administration of numerous inoculations, the issue of those awful combat fatigues which had become all the rage for troops being posted abroad and for a number of talks about the terms of the armistice which we were about to police. We were told something about the countries we would be assigned to and were assured that administrative support had been arranged for us. It soon became painfully obvious that the briefing officers were not very knowledgeable; anyone who had read recent issues of *Time* magazine could have covered the subject just as well. It also became obvious that not much had been done to organise logistic support for us. We were briefed about the need for us to perform our duties in a strictly neutral manner, about not taking any type of weapon (even a pen knife was deemed unacceptable), and not to take any civilian clothes. It was not long after our arrival in Indochina that we found that these admonitions were unworkable and they were soon more or less ignored. It was well-nigh impossible to refrain from any social contacts with members of the former enemies. Laundry facilities were minimal and the climatic conditions clearly indicated that we needed more changes of clothing and that comfortable clothing was frequently more appropriate.

I was particularly interested in the moving arrangements. We were told that we would be flown out to Indochina with Hanoi in North Viet Nam as the final destination. There were to be six flights leaving on successive days and that one of the overnight stops would be my native home in Malta. My parents lived there still. They were getting extremely old and frail and this could be my last chance to see them. I explained all this to my Head of Section, a fellow we nicknamed "lizard" because of his striking resemblance to that reptile. My suggestion was that I fly out in draft No.1, stop off in Malta, and then, on the sixth day, pick up flight No.6 and continue my journey to Indochina. The lizard barely heard me out. "Too complicated" was his immediate retort and, with that, there was nothing I could do but accept whatever flight I was assigned to and hope for the best. I later told the Lizard that I had been unable to see my parents because my flight was late in getting to Malta and that both my parents had died while I was in Indochina. He did not show any signs of remorse.

My draft left aboard an RCAF Northstar configured for troop movements as opposed to VIPs. This meant sitting on bucket shaped metal seats with a nut and bolt running right through the middle. There was a row of seats on each side of the aircraft facing inwards. The aisle was packed with wooden crates containing various paraphernalia and there wasn't much room between the tip of my nose and a box labelled STATIONERY.

The Northstar was the workhorse, or should I say mule, of Air Transport Command. It was slow, extremely noisy and would have been the subject of a complaint by an animal rights group had it been carrying cattle. It had a relatively short range and it was necessary to make frequent refuelling stops. The trip to Indochina involved overnight stops in Gander in Newfoundland, the Azores off the coast of Spain, Gibraltar, Malta and, mercifully, a three-day stopover in Cyprus. From there, we flew on to Baghdad in Iraq, Karachi in Pakistan, Calcutta in India, Saigon in South Viet Nam and then on to our final destination, Hanoi in North Viet Nam which was still under French control but which was soon to be handed over to the North Vietnamese. Except for Cyprus, we flew from five in the morning until about three in the afternoon. The theory was that the passengers and crew would have a night's rest between stops. Unfortunately, this theory did not work because, inevitably, someone would notice what seemed like a good night club on the journey from the airport to the hotel. After a quick shower at the hotel, off we would all go for a late night party. By the time we landed in Hanoi we were a sorry looking group as we stumbled down to the tarmac. Major General R.E.A. Morton (Rea as he later came to be affectionately known by the junior officers) was visibly shaken when he saw us. I could hear him thinking "and this is what they sent me to do the job?" Poor Rea; thank goodness we were young and pliable. We quickly recovered.

Hanoi, the capital of North Viet Nam, is located on the western bank of the Red River about 137 kilometers inland from the South China Sea. Because of the fertile soil of the Red River area, Hanoi is an agricultural city although it is also a major centre for communications and industry. It has good rail and road communications to its outport, Haiphong, to Kunming in China and to Saigon in the south.

Hanoi has experienced many political changes. In 1010 it was the capital of the Ly dynasty. In 1902 it served as the French capital of northern Viet Nam. It was occupied by the Japanese from 1940 to 1945.

Hanoi has a population of about eight hundred thousand. It has an almost tropical climate. Its architecture reflects its French heritage. Its broad tree-lined avenues are flanked by prosperous looking villas. It boasts some historical sites such as the Temple of Literature and the Temple of the Trung Sisters. These two women led the rebellion against the Chinese Han dynasty.

There were numerous excellent restaurants, night clubs and good hotels. Sadly, when it was handed over to the Communist government, overnight, it seems, Hanoi was transformed into a dull, grey city. Its streets were lined with decidedly unfriendly sentries with bayonets fixed. Venturing out on to the streets only a few minutes after curfew was not a very safe thing to do. But I am getting ahead of my story. In those early days, Hanoi was a very pleasant city in which to while away one's time. We had been allowed to use the facilities of the Cercle des Officiers (the French officers' club). It had a huge swimming pool where we spent a great deal of time ogling the very chic officers' wives and sundry French nurses. On one occasion, a group of French Foreign Legion officers hosted a party. They had been prisoners-of-war for a lengthy time. They were thin and looked haggard but seemed otherwise fit enough. They had just received their arrears of pay. Some of them had been in captivity for a number of years and the French officers were relatively well paid when they served in Indochina. The Cercle was awash in the finest champagne; we were invited to join in and all had a rollicking good time.

As the days sped by, it became increasingly obvious to us that, after that ungodly rush to get us out to Indochina, we were much too early. The first major problem the Commission faced was the siting of their headquarters. There was no problem in Cambodia and Laos. The obvious choices there were the capitals of the two countries, Phnom Penh in Cambodia and Vientiane in Laos. Viet Nam however presented a problem since to locate the Commission headquarters in either Hanoi in the north or Saigon (now Ho Chi Minh city) in the south could be misconstrued as favouring one side over the other. It was a delicate issue which delayed the organisation of the Commission. In the end, the Commission compromised by establishing its main headquarters in Hanoi and a sub-headquarters in Saigon. There were other difficulties. It was not easy, for example, to recruit adequately qualified interpreters and translators in sufficient numbers. There were five languages to contend with: English, French, Polish, Vietnamese and Laotian. The latter language was particularly troublesome.

While Cambodia and the two Viet Nams presented few problems in the siting of the fixed teams, Laos was problematic. In the end, eleven teams were to be deployed in Laos. They would be sited at various nodal points in the very poor road communication network. These communications were scanty and in very poor shape. Bridges and culverts had been badly damaged in the war and the monsoon rains had washed away long stretches of the roads. The support of teams which were to be deployed was difficult to arrange especially in the northern provinces of Phong Saly and Sam Neua. There were no railway lines and the roads consisted of pony tracks and foot paths over jungle-clad hills. Reliance would have to be placed on slim resources of light aircraft and helicopters. The terrain was inhospitable and there was a totally inadequate supply of buildings to serve as living quarters for the teams. Supplies would have to be air dropped because of a lack of airstrips which could accept even the all-purpose Dakotas. To complicate matters even further, the weather which, at this time of year should have been good, turned very bad. It caused one helicopter crash. The survivors had a three-day trek ahead of them before they could be located and rescued. All this caused delays and it was seemingly a long time before those of us who were Laos bound could be deployed.

The composition and duties of the teams were being developed. In the end it was decided that each team would consist of two officers from each of the three countries. One would be the senior member and was usually in the rank of Lieutenant Colonel or Major and there was to be a junior officer in the rank of Captain. The senior Indian officer would be the team chairman. India also supplied each team with cooks and signallers to keep open the radio communications to the Commission headquarters. The Commission arranged for interpreters although the Polish officers insisted upon their own presumably because they did not trust the one supplied by the Commission. The French supplied, wherever possible, a helicopter or light aircraft. Jeeps painted white and drivers were provided by the local military who were also responsible for our security—a responsibility which the Communist forces took very seriously because it gave them the excuse they needed to prevent us from travelling when and wherever we wanted to. Medical assistance was not available in the northern team sites. All we had was our first aid kit. The sick and injured would have to be evacuated by air as and when suitable air transport became available and flying weather permitted their use.

Generally speaking, the teams were there to "show the flag" which was a strip of white cloth with the letters ICSC stencilled in black. The teams were to act as the eyes and ears of the Commission. They were to keep the headquarters informed of developments in their sphere of responsibility by means of hand-written daily, weekly and special situation reports.

The detailed team responsibilities included the investigation of incidents which may appear to contravene the terms of the Geneva agreement. The teams were also to check the movements of military forces in their area and at the entry points on the frontiers of Laos. The execution of the clauses on the cessation of hostilities and the exchange of prisoners of war and internees were to be supervised by the teams. Each team was to familiarize itself with the surrounding terrain and to establish and maintain contact with the military commanders and senior civilian officials in their area. Team sites were designated as "hard" or "normal." The hard sites were those which were more remote and which did not offer very much by way of what we regarded as basic comforts and congenial surroundings. Phong Saly and Sam Neua were designated hard sites and efforts were made to rotate team personnel at specified periods, usually every six weeks or so, to even out the deployments.

All in all, it looked like a very interesting and challenging job. The security aspect might have looked dicey but at age twenty-nine you feel indestructible. I was anxious to get going to Savannakhet which was to be my first posting.

Mainland Southeast Asia

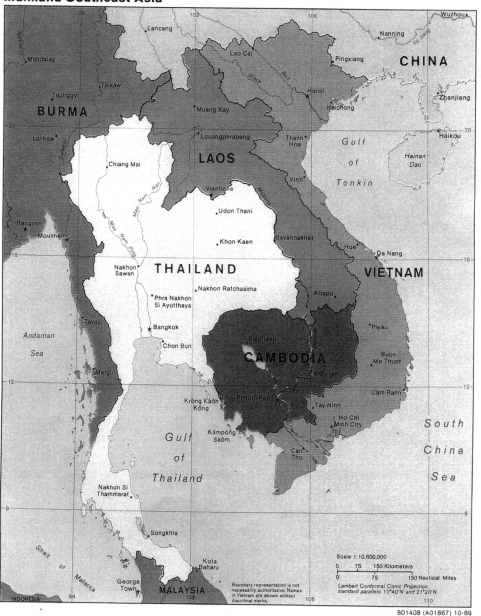

Scale 1:10,600,000

0   75   150 Kilometers

0   75   150 Nautical Miles

Lambert Conformal Conic Projection,
standard parallels 10°40'N and 21°20'N

Boundary representation is not
necessarily authoritative. Names
in Vietnam are shown without
diacritical marks.

801408 (A01867) 10-89

Chapter 2

SAVANNAKHET

ONE BY ONE, team sites had been agreed to by all the parties and logistic arrangements were made. I found myself going to the kingdom of Laos and, more specifically, the town of Savannakhet.

Situated in the rugged mountainous interior of the Indochinese peninsula, landlocked Laos is a land of dense rain forest and towering mountains. It is bordered by Viet Nam in the east, Cambodia in the south, Thailand and Burma in the West and China in the north. It comprises over ninety thousand square miles being roughly seven hundred miles long and two hundred seventy-five miles wide.

For most of the year, Laos is blessed with a warm climate with a wet monsoon period (May to November) and a dry period (December to April). During the monsoon period, it experiences about ten inches of rain per month. The damp climate used to turn all our leather accoutrements green with mould after only a few hours. The country's resources include teak and several minerals such as tin, silver and gold. The Mekong River which flows in a north-south direction forms the border with Thailand. It is one of the largest river systems in eastern Asia and holds promise of substantial hydro-electric potential. The river and its tributaries also provide important arteries of communication between northern and southern Laos and the mountainous interior.

The population of Laos numbers some three million which is sparse by Asian standards. About one million were Laos who were originally inhabitants of southern China and who now form the dominant ethnic group in Laos. They are closely related by customs, religion and appearance to the Thais. The rest of the population is made up of several tribes. The principal ones of these are the Meo, Yao and Kha tribes who were the original inhabitants of the Indochinese peninsula. Generally speaking, these tribes inhabit the mountainous areas of Laos. The two principal cities are Vientiane the administrative capital with a population of about ninety thousand and Luang Prabang the royal capital with a population of about forty thousand. Laos is essentially a country of small towns and villages of some three hundred to five hundred inhabitants. The average number of households within a small town or village range from eight to forty. Houses are usually constructed of bamboo and are built off the ground on wooden piles. The sheltered space beneath the house is used to store tools and to secure livestock at night. Villages are quite isolated especially during the monsoon period when the inter-connecting roads and tracks become difficult if not impassable.

There is hardly any industry in Laos. Its people occupy themselves with farming the rice paddies located in the river valleys or, in the case of the hill people, on patches of ground on the steep-sided hills.

In 1353, Fa Ngoun established the kingdom of Lan Chang—"the kingdom of a million elephants." In the nineteenth century, Laos was taken over by Siam (now Thailand). In 1893 Laos came under French colonial rule. The ruling family of Luang Prabang was declared the royal family of Laos and French rule was exercised through them. Laos gained virtual independence in 1949 and, under the terms of the Geneva Agreement of 1954, it was recognised as a unified, independent and neutral country with a constitutional monarchy. In 1975, the Communist Pathet Lao party deposed the royal family and Laos was declared a Communist People's Republic. Laos had suffered deeply during the anti-colonial war; tens of thousands of battle casualties were suffered and a quarter of its people became refugees.

It is not difficult to understand the strategic importance of Laos. An invader is not searching for riches in Laos; it is however the shortest land route to Thailand, Burma and westward. The domino theory was popular in the fifties and the Western Powers could easily visualise a communist thrust westwards towards India and, perhaps, beyond.

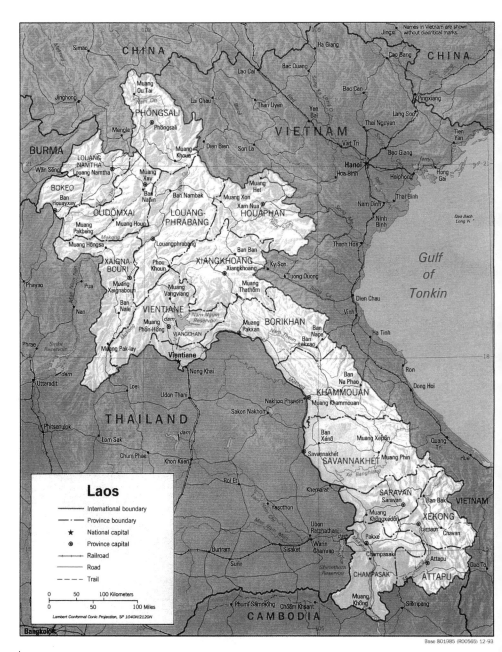

Laos

Laos was an unhealthy place. Malaria, dysentery, typhoid fever, smallpox, tetanus and diphtheria were quite prevalent and infant mortality rates were so high that Laotians did not bother to name their children until they were a year old. It was inevitable that some of us would fall prey to at least one of these diseases. We all took our daily dosages of anti-malarial pills and we had all been adequately inoculated against most of these diseases. Dysentery however was inescapable because of the contaminated drinking water and the use by Laotian farmers of human excrement as manure. We used to wash all our leafy vegetables with permanganate of soda which, while minimising the problem, gave all our salads a purplish tinge making them look most unappetising and a bit like seaweed. The Canadian doctor assigned to the delegation—a fellow with the improbable name of Napoleon Fink—had only two remedies to suggest. For the not-so-bad attacks of dysentery he prescribed sulphur pills. These were about the size of the old English penny and it was necessary to swallow sixteen of them in order to coat the stomach. It was not an easy feat. Severe cases of dysentery, particularly the amoebic kind, meant almost automatically evacuation back to Canada. A friend of mine, Major Sid Lloyd, went to Indochina as a muscular, healthy young man. When I saw him awaiting evacuation to Canada he was skin and bones.

Swimming in any of the rivers was not recommended because of the leeches which attached themselves to any warm body and which could only be persuaded to let go by holding the lighted end of a cigarette close to them. A stroll through the jungle was also not recommended because of the poisonous snakes, particularly the small but quite deadly "branded krait" or, as it came to be called, the "one step" snake because the poison had to be extracted before you took one step. One of our Indian colleagues had a most unpleasant experience with one of these though, thankfully, he was not bitten. While using the biffy, he spotted a krait hanging from the rafters above him. We heard a great scream and the normally quiet-spoken, distinguished looking Sikh major came hurtling out of the biffy with his trousers around his knees. Unkindly, we all had a good laugh not realising that the poor fellow was within a few inches of a very quick and painful death.

Savannakhet was a fair sized town with cobbled streets and a number of quite respectable looking villas built on stilts, a small hotel and a few shops with almost bare shelves. The town's population numbered some two thousand. It was situated astride Route Colonial 19 and about half way up the panhandle of Laos. It was located on the western flank and just south of the demarcation line. The Mekong River flowed through the town. Apart from Route Colonial 19, a number of other routes connect the town to the interior of Laos and central Viet Nam. In a region where communications are, at best, difficult, the town of Savannakhet was an important military and economic hub.

The terms of the Geneva agreement required that military forces would withdraw to their respective zone above and below the 17th parallel. On cessation of hostilities, pockets of French troops found themselves north of the demarcation line while guerrilla groups of the North Vietnamese army were south of it. One of our principal jobs was to check on the withdrawals of these forces so that our headquarters could monitor the overall progress of the execution of the terms of the armistice. We did this by trying to be present at predetermined check points along the withdrawal routes and literally count noses so to speak.

This process was easy where the French forces were concerned. They travelled in orderly road convoys and the officer in charge of the convoy prepared a neat list of the number of troops and the weapons contained in each vehicle. We also received plenty of notice of these movements and we were able to be at the prescribed check-point ready to do our monitoring. The Viet Minh forces however were a totally different kettle of fish. They straggled through remote jungle paths carrying their sick and wounded on makeshift stretchers and all their stores and weapons were hand-carried. Sometimes, elephants were used to carry the heavier loads strapped to their backs. These columns did not seem to be in radio contact with anyone and it is not surprising that their superiors were often genuinely unaware of their progress and hence unable to give us adequate notice of their movement. Setting up check points along these jungle routes often involved an arduous jeep journey to the end of the track and then a long march along jungle trails. Frequently we got to the check point too late to do any kind of an effective job. When we did manage to make contact with one of these columns, we were amazed at the apparently high morale and tenacity of these soldiers. Perhaps the fact that they were going home after heaven knows how many months of living and fighting in the jungle spurred them on.

It was also important for us to "hold court" whenever we received a complaint from the Laotian civilians. These complaints usually

The
Savannakhet
market

revolved around the alleged abduction of males of military age who would be forced to join the columns and return with them to communist territory for indoctrination and enlistment in the ranks of the Vietnamese army. The six of us would sit behind two six-foot tables and interview complainants through our interpreters. It was a long process because it usually involved several languages and, I suspect, indifferent interpreters. The complainant would speak Laotian. This had to be translated into French and, from French, into English and Polish. To complicate matters, the Poles routinely refused to accept the word of the Laotian-French interpreter. They had to have their own interpreter. The whole process often degenerated into heated arguments about who said what. Once all the evidence had been collected discussions ensued about the content and wording of the report to the Commission headquarters who would either accept the report or direct us to re-open the investigation. The Polish members usually ended up demanding that they submit a minority report. The wonder of all this is that anything ever came of it. It took time and patience but, I firmly believe, our investigations occasionally succeeded in re-uniting a family with an abducted member, usually the bread-winner.

Cartoon by Grassick

Indo-China truce-team members feel like castaways on a desert island.

Blair Fraser's impression of an ICSC team

These "court sessions" were not without humour. The French-Polish interpreter was a wizened little man who strongly resembled Jimmy Durante. He had a very long nose and we promptly nick-named him "Jimmy." He readily answered to the name and was quite proud of the fact that he had been likened to an American film star. He was a difficult person however when it came to doing his job. Absolutely nothing deterred him from the most meticulous examination of the wording of the evidence given by the witnesses and the nuances which their evidence, in his opinion, imparted. The only time we caught him off guard was when a particular complainant appeared to give evidence. She was a statuesque young woman who appeared before us completely topless. Jimmy's eyes nearly popped out of his head when she swayed sensuously up to our table. His attention became riveted on the complainant's upper torso; he was obviously not keeping his Colonel informed of the proceedings. I believe this particular court session was one of the very few which resulted in unanimity without the bother of a Polish dissenting vote.

Life for us in Savannakhet was quite leisurely when we weren't travelling to some remote jungle check point or holding court. Savannakhet had not been the site of many pitched battles. The buildings were relatively unscarred and there were no minefields to clear in the area. Our off-duty hours were filled with a bridge game after dinner, a long walk along the banks of the Mekong river and the odd drink at the hotel's bar. Our daily chores included keeping up an adequate supply of safe drinking water which we hauled from the river, stored in a large canvas bag hanging from one of the rafters and chlorinating it with our supply of pills. Keeping ourselves clean was difficult because there were no shops from which to buy such rudimentary things as soap, toothpaste and disinfectant. Mail, both outgoing and incoming, was a very real problem. The authorities at Canadian Forces Headquarters had declined the French offer to provide postal facilities insisting instead that we would use the virtually non-existent civilian postal services. The situation was vexing to those of us who had families in Canada; it was especially troublesome to me because of the advanced stage of pregnancy in which I had left my wife.

I shared a billet with Lieutenant Colonel Jeff Baker of the Royal Canadian Regiment, two Indian officers, two Polish officers and a number of interpreters. In a short while we became quite friendly although there was always a strain in our relationship with the Polish officers. The senior Indian officer, a Lieutenant Colonel, used to tell us about his country. I remember him telling me that, when he got home from work, his wife used to insist on washing his feet. He was quite embarrassed about this but she insisted that it was her right to do so. I somehow could not imagine that happening in my household.

Our billet was in a villa which, though sparsely furnished, was reasonably comfortable. We had our meals at the only remaining European-style restaurant owned and operated by a somewhat formidable French lady who seemed to take a liking to Canadians. It is too bad that her food did not reflect this. Everything, it seems, was marinated in a strong garlic concoction making it difficult to differentiate between the various types of meats on the menu. Wishing to at least avoid garlic for breakfast we struggled to explain that we would like boiled eggs. We finally discovered the French equivalent called *oeuf-a-la-coq*. Our five-man ration packs containing canned and pre-packaged foods were designed to be eaten when cooking, for one reason or another, was not feasible. They were supposed to be kept for emergency situations but they came in very handy. We dug into ours quite frequently when Madame's dishes were particularly venomous.

Although we were not supposed to mix socially with either side, we developed a pleasant relationship with a fellow by the name of Zeke Paddock. He was a very tall, stern looking man who lived in a palatial villa on the bank of the Mekong River. The sunset views were magnificent from his veranda. Zeke worked for the American embassy and he pumped us for news most of the time. I suspect he was with the CIA but I do not know that for sure. Perhaps he liked our company. The Poles were never invited for a drink at Zeke's villa. We also developed a good relationship with the officers of a Foreign Legion battalion which was stationed in our area and which had not yet received orders to move. The Legion officers had literally seen it all. They had served in Indochina for a long time and had managed to survive a great deal of the fighting; they lived very much for the present. I struck up a friendship with two of the young Legion officers who persuaded me to go with them on a black panther hunt. They were armed to the teeth for these excursions and had strong flashlights strapped to their helmets. They rode in a jeep and I managed to edge myself on to the back shelf of the vehicle. I of course did not have any weapon so I was quite defenceless. Suddenly the jeep would come to a screeching halt when the two Legionnaires spotted what they thought were a pair of green eyes in the jungle. At this, they leaped out of the jeep and ran into the jungle leaving me shivering with fright in the complete darkness. This was repeated until, at last, they bagged a scruffy looking animal. Needless to say, I declined their second invitation for a black panther hunt.

A Tabor battalion was also stationed nearby. It was an Algerian unit with French officers. One evening, they asked us out to what we would call a mess dinner. They specified that we could each bring a lady guest and I invited a rather colourful French nurse who everybody called Madame Plume. She had been parachuted into Dien Bien Phu at the height of the battle and had been taken prisoner by the Viet Minh. She was also much decorated for bravery under fire. Madame Plume was not exactly a beauty but she was the only Caucasian woman within two hundred miles. I considered myself quite lucky when she accepted my invitation. Dinner at the Tabor battalion was held in a huge tent with big, soft pillows strewn around on the floor in a semi-circle. The officers and their guests squatted on these pillows and drank numerous glasses of a strong Algerian wine. Two Tabors dressed in flowing white robes they called a "bournousse" marched in with a freshly killed and skinned lamb impaled on their fearsome lances. The Commanding Officer was invited to inspect the carcass. When he expressed his satisfaction the soldiers marched smartly out to barbecue the lamb over an open fire. Perhaps it was the wine, but barbecueing did not seem to take very long. The beautifully cooked lamb was eaten with the fingers. A delicious piece was stripped off by each dinner guest, dipped into a bowl of a sort of corn, savoured and washed down with some more of that potent Algerian red wine. It was delicious and, as the evening wore on, the tent got more and more noisy. When the meal was over, the battalion brothel of eight quite good looking Arab women entertained us with dancing. I would estimate that they were in their late thirties and had been with the battalion for several years. They were dressed in filmy, multi-coloured veils and they danced as if they were straight out of a Hollywood movie. I learned that these were not there just as a sexual outlet for the soldiers; they also provided a homey touch by doing housewifely chores such as making curtains for the barracks, sewing torn clothing, cooking, doing the laundry and attending to minor cuts and bruises. I thought it was a very sensible arrangement especially when the battalion medical officer told me that there had not been a case of venereal disease among the men for several years.

In spite of Savannakhet's attractions, I was quite relieved when the magic word "rotation" began to get around. Rotation involved moving each of us from one team site to another after six to eight weeks. It was a brilliant idea. It gave us a better overview of the country, it broke the monotony of life in a very small community and, by sharing the "good" and "bad" sites, it contributed to morale. A few Canadians had already broken under the strain of life in Indochina and had been or were about to be returned to Canada. Some of the team sites were quite rough insofar as living conditions were concerned. They lacked what we would regard as basic necessities such as running water, sanitary facilities, electricity and any means of communication to the outside world. Others were not only rough but very boring because they were being obstructed by the Viet Minh from doing their work. I supposed that the Viet Minh were not anxious to let us see what there was to be seen. Liquor supplies began to flow in from Hong Kong at ridiculously low prices and that, I heard, was the undoing of one or two of our colleagues. At any rate, the rotation orders arrived and I was to go as General Staff Officer Grade 3 (the most junior) at the Canadian Delegation headquarters in Vientiane.

The Commission had chartered aircraft to ferry us around. The two French airlines which operated in Indochina were called Air France and Aigle Azur (blue eagle). Now these were not what you would call proper airlines. at least in Indochina. They employed pilots who seemed positively ancient to me and who had the disconcerting habit of flying their passenger aircraft a little like frustrated fighter pilots. The aircraft they flew were quite old and looked beaten up. One of the aircraft was actually a 1930 vintage biplane called a Dragon. It looked as if it were held together by bailing wire and fervent prayers. We had a rather wry Movements Corporal who acted as a sort of travel agent. He validated your travel authorisation and, where possible, assigned you to a specific airline. Our Movements Corporal had a rather twisted sense of humour. He would look at you with a twinkle in his eyes and ask "What's it to be today Sir, take a chance with Air France or dead for sure with Aigle Azur?" It was not always very funny and it began to wear thin as you observed the sixty-or-so-year-old pilot with his cap on the back of his head, leaning against the lower wing of the Dragon, smoking a big cigar just inches away from the highly flammable aviation spirit being pumped into the tank.

I finally settled on an Air France "Beaver" because I knew that these aircraft were built in Canada and I was soon winging my way over the jungle towards Vientiane. I rode in the co-pilot's seat and tried to observe every move the pilot made in the vain hope that if he should have a heart attack, I would attempt to land the wretched thing. I do not suppose that I would have made it but it was comforting to know that I could do *something* in an emergency. In retrospect, I do not suppose that the pilot was all that old; he only seemed to be to a twenty-nine-year-old like myself!

The pilot had been in Indochina for several years and knew the country inside out. He was a very interesting man and he described the landmarks to me as we flew over them. While wishing he would pay a little more attention to the controls than to me, I did find out from him why parts of the jungle always seemed to be on fire. He explained that the Meo tribes were a nomadic people who specialized in growing poppies from which they made opium. They would set an area of the jungle on fire so as to clear enough ground for their crop. The ash acted as a fertiliser. They planted their seed in the open ground and, when the crop was harvested and the opium extracted, they would move on to some other patch of ground. It was a classic example of the "slash and burn" method of agriculture practised by nomadic people in the Americas, Africa, Indonesia and Southeast Asia. Essentially, it is a rotation system. Farmers chop the undergrowth away, kill the trees by cutting off a strip of bark around the trunk of the tree and then set it on fire. After four or five years, the soil loses much of its fertility and the area is abandoned in favour of a new clearing. This form of shifting cultivation is considered to be a form of subsistence agriculture which results in the production of sufficient food stuffs to sustain a family. With opium of course, the crop is destined for special markets.

The Meo tribes were a very colourful people. The men wore a garment that closely resembled a Scottish kilt. Their legs were encased in colourful woollen stockings without any feet. They carried their opium in short pieces of hollow bamboo and they traded the opium to the Chinese shop keepers for such things as axes and lanterns. The Meo women went completely topless but they wore numerous necklaces made out of bits of metal and bone. They were handsome women with high cheek bones, beautiful eyes and quite graceful figures.

The ride to Vientiane was mercifully short and we soon bumped our way down the runway and taxied over to the shack which passed for a terminal building. A jeep and driver were there to meet me and, in a few minutes, I was at the front door of an edifice which I shall never forget called The Setha Palace Hotel.

Chapter 3

VIENTIANE

LAOS HAS TWO CAPITALS, a royal capital at Luang Prabang and an administrative capital in Vientiane. If there was any action at all in Laos, it would have occurred in Vientiane with its population of two hundred thousand.

Laos is a mushroom shaped country lying roughly on a northwest-southeast axis. Vientiane is near the top of the stem of the mushroom on the 20th parallel of latitude. The city is built on the north bank of the Mekong River which is only navigable to small craft at Vientiane. The river forms the border with Thailand and ferries cross it at Vientiane. The terrain around Vientiane is flat and open. Vientiane lies astride a number of highways, the principal one of which links Savannakhet in the south, through Vientiane and to Luang Prabang in the north.

Vientiane was founded in the thirteenth century and came under Siamese (Thai) control in 1778. The French took the city over in 1899 and made it the seat of the French governor of Laos. There is an international airport, a university, a number of colleges, libraries and museums. The Buddhist temple of That Luang was founded in 1586. The city is home to a number of light industries and a dam to the north of the city generates enough power to meet its needs. The countryside is fertile; farmers grow rice and corn and tend cattle.

The Setha Palace Hotel was home to the junior staff posted to the Canadian Delegation Headquarters. It had obviously known better days and one could only imagine the glittering affairs that took

The Villa Canada

The Setha Palace Hotel

place in its spacious dining room in French colonial days. War and neglect had taken their toll and the old lady was showing it badly. It was a large two-storey edifice built around an open courtyard. The hallways were wide but quite devoid of furniture, carpets and window dressing. One's footsteps echoed along the hallways and the dim lighting gave them a ghostly air. The bedrooms were also quite large but very sparsely furnished. A huge four-poster bed with mosquito netting, a bureau for clothing, an armoire and perhaps a chair or two. The floor was completely bare as were the windows. The room I was assigned to boasted a private bathroom but the fixtures were rather rudimentary and were not always in service. A small concrete enclosure served as the shower room. It had green slime on the walls and was the haunt of large, fat green lizards. A tall clay urn stood in the corner of the shower room. It was filled with water which had obviously been stagnating for some time. A cloud of mosquitoes lived quite happily on the surface of the water.

I soon learned the purpose of the urn. The hotel's water supply depended on a pump driven by a gasoline engine which was installed in the middle of the courtyard under a tree. The pump was tended by a young Laotian who, I swear, knew the precise moment that a hotel guest had lathered up for a shower. At that precise moment, the attendant would shut the pump down. The drill then was to wrap a towel around one's middle, pad out to the veranda and plead with the boy to start up the pump. The pleas fell on deaf ears until the victim had thrown down the requisite number of piastre notes. This had a magic effect on the boy who strolled lazily to the pump and re-started the thing. Slowly, the water would start trickling down from the shower head but, by this time, the lather had caked solidly. Of course all this could have been avoided by using the stagnant water in the urn to wash away the lather but one paid a price for this in mosquito bites. The water supply in that hotel was so meagre that the secretary of our delegation asked us to save our ration of soda water so that she could wash her hair. We drank our scotch neat.

We ate our meals at the Villa Canada just around the corner from the Setha Palace. The villa became the officers' mess. The top floor provided somewhat more luxurious sleeping quarters for the senior staff while the ground floor housed the lounge and dining room. Our meals were prepared by a couple of Laotian cooks who worked out of a sort of shed at the bottom of the back garden. Colonel John Delamere presided over all this and, in true army fashion, promptly delegated all the lousy jobs to the junior staff. I inherited the unenviable job of Mess Secretary which meant that I was to see that all ran to Colonel Delamere's satisfaction. It was not an easy job because he was a hard task master. Everything had to run smoothly in a country where nothing ever ran smoothly. He wanted everything to be ship-shape and was always inspecting whatever came into his view. He thought it unseemly to yell at the waiters hanging around the cook house to come and serve the next dish. He directed me to purchase a bell with which to summon the staff. This was sensible enough except that that there did not seem to be a single bell for sale in Vientiane. I hunted all over town and finally found a dimly lit Chinese shop where they sold wooden cow bells. The bell I purchased did not tinkle to Colonel Delamere';s satisfaction. In fact it clonked rather than tinkled. I think they eventually had to send to Saigon for a suitable replacement.

Colonel J.M. Delamere was a handsome, distinguished looking man who reminded me of the monocled colonel who once appeared on the English Kensitas cigarette package. He was the perfect clothes horse with perfectly fitting uniforms which were always beautifully pressed. He wore the ribbons of numerous campaign medals on his left breast and these, with the red gorget patches on his collar befitting his rank, made him look very colourful. He and Lieutenant Colonel

Colonel Delamere ladles the soup at the dinner table at Villa Canada

Jack Reynolds, a gunner officer, managed to import from Hong Kong beautifully tailored white mess uniforms which they had designed themselves (there was no such authorised dress to my knowledge). How they managed to keep those whites clean and pressed was a mystery to all of us because there were no dry cleaners in Vientiane. Our boys washed our uniforms in the Mekong River which was quite brown. Those crisp white uniforms put our crumpled issue fatigues to shame.

Colonel Delamere was also a stickler for discipline at the dinner table. As soon as the dessert and coffee were served, he would start recounting various experiences he had had when he commanded a battalion of the Queen's Own Rifles of Canada. He would ramble on endlessly, forgetting that he was being repetitive. He would not allow anyone to leave the table until he saw fit to rise. It was difficult to stifle our yawns and one of us, Captain Sy Gibson of the Service Corps, had the temerity to fall asleep and snore rather loudly at the table. He made himself thoroughly unpopular with the Colonel.

The headquarters building was located just a few minutes walk from Villa Canada. It consisted of a large, one-storey bungalow divided up into offices. I shared an office with Captain Gilles Perodeau, the Canadian Guards. We became very good friends. I am pleased to say that our friendship has borne the test of time because, to this day, we keep in touch. Gilles has been very helpful in the preparation of this book providing me with all sorts of

Gilles Perodeau in his "whites"

Tennis with Gilles Perodeau

The Pam Pam night club

photographs and aides memoire. He and I were about the same age, we had the same sense of humour, we played tennis together and we went out frequently in the evenings.

The staff quickly settled down to our duties. I was primarily responsible for the collection and collation of intelligence. I was asked to focus my attention on estimating the battle-worthiness of the Royal Laotian army. While the Geneva agreement brought peace to Laos, nobody was under any illusions about the fragile nature of this state of affairs especially in the light of the ambitions of the Communist Pathet Lao forces in the north. It therefore became necessary for the Commission to have an idea of the defensive capabilities of the Royal Laotian forces.

Some information was already available in our files but it was scattered all over the place and needed to be compiled and arranged into a co-ordinated picture. The French military mission to Laos also had plenty of information but this too had to be sorted out, and analysed. We were also invited to observe military training exercises carried out by the Laotian army. We needed to record and assess these from the point of view of our own measures of the battle worthiness of the units involved.

In general, we concluded that the Laotian defence force could not, unaided, contain a determined North Vietnamese thrust into Laos for very long. The Laotian air force consisted of six or seven light aircraft which, at most, could be used for casualty evacuation provided the French would provide ground support for the air strips. The Laotian navy consisted of a few light speed boats which were capable of patrolling only the most important stretches of the waterways. The bulk of the army was about thirty five thousand men hastily organised into a number of battalion-sized units. They had only recently been established, they had no battle experience and their leadership was poor. They were skimpily supported by a few tanks, a few artillery pieces and some logistic units. The manpower reserves from which this army could draw were not in the least bit warlike. While the young soldiers who made up the rank and file were a happy-go-lucky sort who would put up with all sorts of deprivations, they were not by nature and tradition aggressive enough to withstand the rigours of battle. The Laotian government desperately needed time in which to toughen their ground forces and to build up some semblance of a defence capability provided they were helped by the French fifteen hundred-man liaison mission.

Quite apart from the humanitarian aspects of the cease fire, these conclusions highlighted the importance of a reasonably lengthy period of stability during which the Laotian government could build up a defensive capability. Time was of the essence and both sides knew it all too well. While this may sound as retrospective grand-standing, while we were there, it was unlikely that the Communists in the North would launch any offensive operations into Laos.

The ranking French officer in Laos, Colonel Huré, headed the French Military Mission to the Royal Laotian forces. It was necessary for our Senior Military Advisor, Major General Morton, to pay a courtesy call on Colonel Huré in order to pave the way for our intelligence gathering activities and as a general exchange of military courtesies. General Morton asked me to accompany him.

"I am going to pay Colonel Huré a visit tomorrow morning. A courtesy more or less, but there are some other things I want to bring up with him. I want you to come with me. Please pick me up at 1045 hours tomorrow."

"Very good sir," I responded. "Is there anything you particularly want me to do?" I asked.

"Just keep your ears open and your mouth shut," was the uncharacteristic reply although it was said in a kindly way.

I knew General Morton's degree of fluency in the French language. It was high schoolish to say the least. I had also exchanged pleasantries with Colonel Huré at a recent cocktail party and remembered that his grasp of the English language was just as rudimentary. I pinned my hopes on Colonel Huré providing an interpreter but prepared myself for the worst. My own knowledge of the French language was not very advanced.

Colonel Huré's office was typical of the man. It was uncluttered, comfortable yet austere. Huré was a cavalry officer with a soldierly bearing. He was dressed in a neatly pressed khaki uniform much adorned with campaign ribbons. There was no one else in the room. No sooner had Colonel Huré made us comfortable than General Morton's opening remark confirmed my worst fears.

"Nous sommes chaud aujourd'hui," he blurted out, referring to the heat of the day. The correct expression would have been "Il fait chaud aujourd'hui." To say "nous sommes chaud" meant we were *sexually* hot.

Colonel Huré was too much of a gentleman to laugh out loud but a smile lingered on his lips. However, he was obviously taken aback by General Morton's opening gambit.

"Oui, mon general. Il fait tres chaud," he agreed. "Prenez-vous une tasse de caffe Algerien?"

We nodded agreement and a soldier appeared with three steaming hot cups of very strong coffee. General Morton was a little awkward socially and promptly spilled some of his coffee onto the front of his tunic.

"Excuse moi," he said blushing "J'ai spillez mon coffee." There is of course no such French word as "spillez" and this time the Colonel was a little less restrained.

General Morton tried to steer the conversation to the business of the day but quickly saw that he was getting way over his head. He turned to me and asked me to translate. The Colonel did the same and I soon found myself doing a great deal more than just keeping my ears open and my mouth shut.

It was a measure of General Morton's gentility that he never reproached me for going beyond what his original instructions to me had been. Rea became very dear to me. He was very much a soldier's general and had a real feeling for the humanities involved in commanding men. He was the first one to send me a signal of condolence when he heard that both my parents had died and he was the first to go out and rough it with the troops in the most out-of-the-way team sites. During the latter part of my tour of duty in Vientiane, a signal arrived belatedly informing me that my second son Mark was born on 16 November. Mother and son were doing fine. It took the signal almost four weeks to reach me. Rea was the first to congratulate me and, to celebrate the occasion, he took me and several other junior officers out to a champagne dinner. We toasted Mark's health rather often I remember. It was typical of Rea—a major general—to do this kind of thing for a mere captain.

Rea was an avid photographer and always wore at least two, sometimes three, cameras around his neck. He was not a very successful photographer and kept forgetting to remove the cover from the lens. He was also a naturalist and wrote a pamphlet about the flora and fauna of Laos. He was a collector and had his eye on acquiring one of the wooden crossbows the Laotians fashioned out of teak. He asked me to go out and buy one. Like the bell, these were hard to find. I finally accosted a tall, old Laotian wearing a flowing robe and sporting a long, white beard. He was carrying one of those crossbows. Once again, we had a problem of communication. I spoke no Laotian and he spoke no recognisable language. I rather gathered that he would

NOTICE TO ALL STAFF MEMBERS

MEMORIAL SERVICE

Since the Commission opened in Laos several of the members of the Canadian Delegation have received word of the death of parents in Canada.

In memory of these deceased parents Mr. Mayrand has arranged for a requiem mass to be said at the Cathedral at 7.30 a.m. on Wednesday, June 8. Mass will be said for the repose of the souls of the following:

Mrs. Brennan	Mother of Lt. Col. Brennan
Mrs. Kohler	Mother of Captain Kohler
Mr. and Mrs. de Domenico	Parents of Captain de Domenico
Mrs. Arseneau	Mother of Sgt. Arseneau

Notice of a requiem mass in memory of my parents

I.A.F.U-4009 (Small), FOR COMM CEN/SIGNALS USE	**MESSAGE FORM**	NUMBER 213032

PRECEDENCE—ACTION "PRIORITY"	PRECEDENCE—INFO DEFERRED	DATE—TIME GROUP 182204 Z	MESSAGE INSTRUCTIONS

FROM CANARMY

TO INTERNATIONAL SUPERVISORY COMMISSION
CANADIAN DELEGATION
VIENTIANE
INDO-CHINA

INFO ZEN/RCSA (AA) PT

PREFIX	GR 26
SECURITY CLASSIFICATION	UNCLASS
ORIGINATORS NUMBER	ADM10 173
SPECIAL INSTRUCTIONS	

ADVISE SB 3296 CAPT JEG DC DOMENICO SON BORN 16 NOV 54 MOTHER AND BABY WELL (.) RCASE (AA) OUR A 796 REFERS

Page....of....Pages	REFERS TO MESSAGE	CLASSIFIED [ ] YES [ ] NO	DRAFTERS NAME	OFFICE	TEL No.

FOR OPRS USE	R	DATE 21	TIME 2359	SYSTEM W/T	OPERATOR BHATI	D	DATE	TIME	SYSTEM	OPERATOR	RELEASING OFFICERS SIGNATURE

RANK COPIED BY SAM

Notification of Mark's birth

consider selling the crossbow but I got the idea he wanted a thousand piastres for it. We bargained for a long time using our fingers and our hands in a slashing motion to indicate reductions in price. The old man finally gave up in what was obviously disgust and, with a shrug of his shoulders, he ambled off down the road still carrying his crossbow. These proceedings had been followed by my French driver. He explained to me that the old man was only asking one piastre (a few cents at the official rate of exchange). I eventually found one in a sort of hardware store for a very reasonable price and proudly presented it to the general, who was delighted.

Our contact with the Polish officers were minimal. Occasionally, we or they, threw a cocktail party where the atmosphere was always strained and distant. I did manage to strike up a relationship with one of the younger Polish officers. Bogdan was twenty seven years old, young for a captain in the Polish army. He was the aide to the Polish Senior Military Advisor and had graduated from a Warsaw university in the social sciences. He spoke English quite well and, judging by his bearing and the awkward way in which he wore his uniform, he was quite new to the army. He enjoyed the company of westerners and sometimes spoke guardedly of the different standards of living that prevailed in North America and Poland. He was an avowed communist when it came to talking politics and he was obviously a member of the Communist party back home. He was also a bit of a thespian. One day he invited us to the Polish villa for an evening of amateur theatre. He and his friends had worked hard to rig up a makeshift stage, acquire the props and paint the scenery. It was supposed to represent the sitting room of a nineteenth century "impoverished nobleman" of Polish society. After the customary glass or two of vodka, we were ushered to our seats to watch a play entitled "The Wedding." Bogdan had gone to the trouble of writing an English summary of the play so that we might be better able to follow the Polish dialogue. The story was set in the middle of the nineteenth century and concerned an impoverished nobleman who, like his contemporaries, traded on their inherited titles to lure "rich bourgeois" girls into marriage. The "snobbistic" aspirations of these girls apparently made them fair game. The play was written by somebody named Nicholas Gogol who was no doubt in good standing with the Communist Party back home. It was described as an "incredible occurrence in two acts."

Maj. General Morton, Colonel Delamere and Lt. Colonel Reynolds

Mr. Nehru visits
with H.E. Mr. Leon
Mayrand

The author on the office verandah

The suitor, a counsellor at the royal court, was described as an old bachelor who was lazy and indecisive. Beset by financial problems, he consults with a marriage broker who recommends the twenty-seven year old daughter, Agafya, of a rich merchant. Agafya is portrayed as a naive person and the play strongly implied that, until she met the nobleman, she was still a virgin. Things progress well for both parties particularly for the nobleman who seduces Agafya. He then gets cold feet and, at the eleventh hour, he leaps out of the ground floor window, hails a taxi and vanishes. The play came to a merciful end with Agafya crying out in shame.

Had it not been for the frequent replenishment of our vodka glasses, the play would have been exceedingly difficult to sit through especially as the English summary was not of much help in following the Polish dialogue. We applauded politely however, thanked our hosts and privately vowed that we would avoid any further cultural contacts with our Polish friends.

One of the nicest people in Vientiane was undoubtedly the Senior Military Advisor to the Indian ambassador. General Guyani was a tall, handsome, soldierly-looking fellow who lived in some splendour in a private villa. He was still very British in his outlook and favoured the Canadians over, I suspect, his own officers. He threw the occasional dinner party at his villa to which he invited a few Canadian junior officers. After a tasty curry dinner, two lovely Indian ladies dressed in those beautiful saris would strum on a guitar-shaped instrument and sing haunting Indian folk songs. General Guyani translated the words of each song. One such song told a story of the Romeo and Juliet type. It told the story of a beautiful young Indian lady of a high Brahmin caste who fell in love with a servant in her father's home. The young man was an "untouchable," one of India's millions to whom the most menial tasks are assigned. The lovers' encounters in the garden of the young woman's home were observed by the head servant who, in order to ingratiate himself with his master, reported the matter adding some quite untruthful embellishments. Enraged, the father ordered the young man to return to his remote village. Realising that they would never see each other again, the lovers arrange a final tryst at which they both commit suicide. The story was sung to very haunting music by the young woman's mother who was saddened by the loss of her daughter. It was an old story, I suppose, but it illustrated to me that these sorts of situations occur universally and not just in Venice. These folk songs are called "Rygems" (pronounced RUZLELS). They are sung in Urdu and are filled with sadness and romance. Some of them have their origins in seventh century Persia in the palaces of the Mogul emperors.

We had some very pleasant evenings at General Guyani's villa and these invitations were much sought after. I shall always remember General Guyani kindly and I was thrilled to read about him, years later, when he became the commanding general of the United Nations forces in Palestine in the early sixties.

Perhaps the most astonishing sight I had ever witnessed was at the barracks occupied by a Sikh signals battalion. It was a very warm afternoon and the sun was blazing down. Squatting in beautifully straight lines in three ranks on the dirt floor of the parade square were several hundred bare-headed Sikh soldiers dressed in loin cloths. It was their day for washing and drying their waist long hair and beards. They had evidently washed their hair in the barracks and were then marched out to the parade square where they were ordered to squat. They were in their normal company formations with each of their Company Sergeant Majors squatting in their usual front and centre positions. Not a sound was to be heard and the men sat rigidly to attention. When the Battalion Sergeant Major was satisfied that the sun had had enough time to do its job, he barked a brief command in Hindi. The men leapt to their feet ready to be marched smartly back to their quarters. Our equivalent to this was the weekly "make'n mend" afternoon when we were allowed to lounge about in our barracks, mend our clothing, darn our socks, spit and polish our boots and accoutrements. It seemed that the Sikh version was much more disciplined and probably more effective.

One of the highlights of a night out in Vientiane was an hour or two at the only night club. It was called "The Pam Pam" after the brand name of the cans of grapefruit (*pamplemousse*) juice which some enterprising French businessman had imported in huge quantities into Vientiane., The Pam Pam was not much of a place; it was a bamboo shack with a long bar, a few tables and chairs and the usual coterie of dance hostesses. I went there one evening with Jack Thurrott, the political advisor to the Canadian delegation. Jack was a tall, red-faced man with a fund of stories about the many postings he had enjoyed all over the world as one of Canada's Foreign Service Officers. He was fun to be with. For once the table talk did not centre on the army, soldiering and all that. Jack and I were having a pleasant evening. I had in mind however that the following morning I would have to wake up early to go out on a reconnaissance in the nearby jungle. I bid Jack goodnight and went back to my billet at the Setha Palace at a reasonable hour.

The next morning, I strolled over to Villa Canada for breakfast. Colonel Delamere was already at the table. He nearly fell off his chair when he saw me.

"I thought you were dead," he exclaimed. "Weren't you with Jack Thurrott last night?"

I said that I was but that I had left early. Apparently Jack stayed on a bit longer and, on his way back, his jeep overturned, killing him instantly.

Jack Thurrott's coffin being placed on the Dakota for the journey to Saigon

"We are shipping Jack's body to Saigon today and I want you to be his escort." It was necessary to act fast in this part of the world because there was no facility for embalming in Vientiane and the body had either to be buried quickly or shipped to Saigon for proper handling. There was some confusion about who would take responsibility for Jack's remains once we got to Saigon. He could not be buried until somebody came forward from his next-of-kin and, at the time, Jack was going through a divorce. Eventually, his parents in Canada stepped in.

We loaded the coffin on to a cargo Dakota which, I quickly noted, had no seats in it at all. It was going to be a three-hour flight to Saigon and there was nothing left for me to do but to perch as delicately as possible on a corner of the coffin. I started reading the book I had hastily packed. It was a hugely funny book called "No Time For Sergeants" which I was in the midst of reading. Every now and then I had to restrain my need to laugh out loud which, I thought, would be disrespectful. I soon rationalised that Jack would want nothing better than a happy escort to his last resting place.

About half way to Saigon, the French pilot decided to enter into the festive spirit of the thing and insisted on circling very low over the ruins of the lost city of Angkor in the Kampuchean (Cambodian) jungle. He told me the story of the French naturalist Henri Mounot who, in the mid-1800s, while searching for rare birds and butterflies in the jungle, stumbled on the

Colonel Delamere and Jack Thurrott

mysterious temple of Angkor Wat—a huge stone building topped by five lotus-shaped towers. When news of Mounot's discovery reached France, a team of scholars went out to Cambodia and found the city of Angkor which, from the ninth to the fifteenth centuries, was the capital of the Khmer Kingdom which stretched from Viet Nam to the Bay of Bengal. The city's most impressive monuments are the temples of Angkor Wat. These were built by Suryavarman II in the twelfth century, and the Bayon at Angkor Thom built by Javarman VII in the early thirteenth century. The city was once a vast metropolis with roads, canals, towers, temples, galleries, terraces, reservoirs and giant stone statues. It was the religious and administrative centre of the Khmer Kingdom until it was sacked by the invading Thai armies.. It remained deserted and largely forgotten for four hundred years until its discovery by Henri Mounot.

I suppose I should have asked because I was told absolutely nothing about what to do with Jack's remains when I got to Saigon. Fortunately, someone signalled ahead and a Saigon undertaker was waiting at the airport and took charge of things. As the hearse drove away, I saluted Jack, hopped into my waiting jeep and was driven into Saigon where a room had been reserved for me at the Intercontinental Hotel. It was a very luxurious hotel especially when compared to the Setha Palace.

Having a real hot bath followed by a six-course dinner with wine was almost more than I could believe. After dinner, I bumped into an old friend of mine, Major Maurie Williams of the Royal Canadian Artillery. He escorted me to a tailor's shop where I ordered a white shark-skin suit. The Chinese tailor measured me up and, the very next morning, this dazzling addition to my slender wardrobe was hanging in my closet. It was a perfect fit except for the jacket sleeves. The tailor had only one width of sleeves—narrow. His clients were Chinese and these people had very slender arms. I simply could not get the jacket on. I sent the jacket back to the tailor who soon rectified the problem. In the meantime, I strolled off in shirt sleeves to attend mass at the beautiful cathedral in Saigon. Then it was off to the airport and a flight back to Vientiane trying hard to disguise the contraband I was carrying—a civilian suit.

I needed a haircut soon after returning to Vientiane and I went to a barber who had set up shop on the edge of the sidewalk in downtown Vientiane. He insisted on shaving my ears (a new experience). He also splashed on liberal quantities of a pungent spray. The city sewage runs along the gutter just beneath the sidewalk. The heavy lavender scent and the aroma from the sewage were almost overpowering.

Dizzy and a little sick I was on my way back to the Setha Palace. Along the way, I came across a rather tragic scene. A small Laotian boy had been gored by one of the buffaloes that roamed the streets of Vientiane. Nobody in the crowd of onlookers seemed to be doing anything about it other than gawk at the boy writhing in pain. I lifted the boy on to my jeep and drove as fast as I could to the French army hospital. One of the French doctors severely admonished me for wasting his time on such trivia. I'm afraid I lost my temper and threatened the doctor with a fate worse than death if he did not immediately attend to the boy. Reluctantly, he did so. The incident struck me as typical of the diminishing value of human life as one travelled farther and farther east. I later heard that the boy recovered from his wound.

One of the most sought after jobs among the Canadians in Indochina was that of acting as the Diplomatic Courier to New Delhi. The next one was due to go in early December. To my complete astonishment, I was selected. My first stop was Hanoi for a detailed briefing by Frank Ballachey, the First Secretary of our embassy. He kept warning me about the confidentiality of the contents of the bags that I would be carrying. He stressed that diplomatic mail is almost sacred and that under no circumstances apparently, was I to take my eyes off the bags. The first bags would be delivered to me the next morning at my hotel. Before leaving for New Delhi I had a free evening which I spent in the company of friends and Colonel James Tedlie, the Deputy Military Advisor in Hanoi, a very jolly fellow who we nick-named Big Jim. We had a drink and a meal. It was clear that the Communists, who had now taken over the administration of Hanoi, had completely transformed the city. They had closed all the entertainment venues up except for one brightly lit place where the entertainment consisted of a lady in baggy pyjamas who sang communist songs. On our way back to our hotel, we noted that the new administration had posted soldiers with fixed bayonets lurking in practically every doorway. Pedestrians were obliged to walk in the middle of the road where the lighting was better. If you veered away from the centre of the road towards the sidewalks, you encountered a very determined-looking young soldier with his bayonet pointing at your stomach. It was almost too much for Big Jim who was not accustomed to being pushed around. There was not much he or we

EXTERNAL AFFAIRS
CANADA

Burmah-Shell Building,
Hanoi.

December 2, 1954

TO WHOM IT MAY CONCERN

This will introduce Captain J. De
DOMENICO of the Canadian Army, who has been
designated as an official diplomatic courier
for the Canadian Government.

All Customs, Immigration, and other
officials of the Republic of India, of the
Republic of South Vietnam, and of those countries
through which Captain de Domenico will be proceeding, are requested to afford him every
courtesy and protection of which he may stand
in need.

Frank G Ballachey
(F.G.Ballachey)

for the Canadian Commissioner,
International Commission for
Supervision and Control in
Vietnam

Designation as an official diplomatic courier

could do about it however and we finally reached our hotel without incident.

The long journey to New Delhi started the next morning. Before climbing aboard the Commission plane, Frank Ballachey again reminded me of the need to keep my eyes on the bags at all times and handed me my special travel documents. These documents consisted of a diplomatic *laissez-passer* which would entitle me to pass through Indian Customs and Immigration without hindrance. They made me feel very important. The first red canvas bag allegedly contained all these top secret documents. It was a very large bag. We flew from Hanoi to Saigon with stops in Vientiane and Phnom Penh in Cambodia. At each stop, someone from the local embassy handed me another bag. I had time for a stop-over in Saigon for a quick meal and a short rest. The next morning, I loaded my four bags on to an Air France Super Constellation—a great improvement on the RCAF Northstar—and we were soon heading for Calcutta where we would transfer to an Air India flight to New Delhi.

I happened to be seated next to a very attractive French lady who was on her way back to France. The red bags at my feet mystified her and we struck up a conversation. Frank Ballachey's strict instructions, though not uppermost in my mind at that particular time, kept ringing in my ears and I tried to be guarded when she asked me about the red bags. I am not sure how I explained them away but the thought did occur to me that here was a modern day Mata Hari and that I could be taken hostage on the way to Calcutta. I had a very ripe imagination I suppose. My fears heightened when the pilot announced that we could not land at Dum Dum airport in Calcutta because of fog and that we would have to land somewhere else at a military airport, refuel and await instructions from Calcutta. The airport was quite dark and seemed deserted; a great place, I thought, for a hostage taking. We learned that the Super Constellation would have to be refuelled by hand because there was no pumper available and that this process might take several hours. We were offered transportation to a local hotel where rooms had been reserved for us. By this time, the lady and I had become quite friendly and she seemed very keen on the hotel idea. By this time also, I had become quite convinced that the lady was not what she seemed to be and that I did have a modern Mata Hari on my hands. I elected to stay with the aircraft and, of course, my bags.

I shall never know what the lady's true intentions were. At the time however, I was feeling quite smug about my ability to resist temptations and to stick with my job. I hope that Frank Ballachey appreciated the sacrifice that I was making.

We waited for five and a half hours for the refuelling process to be completed. As dawn broke, we flew on to Dum Dum airport. The delay meant that I had missed my Air India connection so I was quite relieved when I was met by a member of the staff of the British Consulate in Calcutta. My escort had arranged overnight accommodation for me in Calcutta. I was impressed with the magical effects of my travel documents and whisked through Customs and thence to the British Consulate where I could deposit my bags in the Consulate safe.

The journey from the airport was almost unbelievable. It was several miles long and the road was lined on both sides by masses of people. They were refugees who lived in incredible squalor in tin shanties and ragged tents. Dead animals were everywhere it seemed rotting away in the heat. People were squatting outside their hovels seemingly staring into space or shuffling about aimlessly. The stench was unbearable. It was a relief to arrive at the palatial hotel where turbaned servants catered to every whim of the hotel guests.

The approach of Christmas was very much on my mind so, after a short rest, I decided I would see what I could send home from the bazaar. Getting to the bazaar was an adventure in itself. The moment a hotel guest appeared outside the hotel, he was besieged by hordes of beggars. Many of these carried deformed children in their arms. I was told that these children were purposely deformed in order to evoke pity. The Calcutta police lashed out at these beggars with their long cane sticks clearing the way for the people leaving the hotel. It was all rather unnerving. The bazaar, I was told, had everything from a pin to an elephant. It was hot, crowded, colourful, noisy and bustling.

I had in mind buying a dressing gown for Madge and I soon located a shop where such things were sold. The proprietor grandly waved me to sit on a pile of luxurious carpets while I sipped a cup of Turkish coffee he provided. I looked over the wares which he displayed with a well-practised flourish. The gowns he showed me were magnificent cashmeres with gold embroidery. I had begun to suspect I was not in the right place for my slender pocket book. A particularly beautiful creation caught my gaze and I screwed up the courage to ask the price. The proprietor complimented me on my good taste and said that this particular gown was an exact duplicate of one recently manufactured for Queen Elizabeth. Instantly, I knew I was in the wrong place. I persuaded the shop keeper that I was not in that sort of price bracket. He understood and started showing me less flashy gowns. I finally settled for a moderately priced gown and braced myself for the return journey to the hotel.

The next morning, it was time for me to catch the Air India plane for New Delhi where I hastily made my way to the Canadian High Commission. I located the person who was authorised to take delivery of my red bags and watched as she dumped the contents on to a long, highly polished table. Imagine my surprise when I saw that all that the bags contained were letters which looked suspiciously like Christmas cards and gift wrapped parcels. It detracted somewhat from the feeling of self-sacrifice I had entertained when I resisted Mata Hari's advances.

The return trip to Hanoi was uneventful. I retraced my itinerary touching down in Calcutta, Saigon, Phnom Penh, Vientiane and Hanoi. Once again, I picked up red bags at each of the stops. After a night's rest, I returned to Vientiane where even the Setha Palace felt like home after all my wanderings.

1st February 1955

ອງງຈັບທນທີ........ເດືອນ......໑໙໕໕ ຄນະກັມະການບະຫວາງຊາດ
ກວດຄວາມສງບໄນປະເທດລາວ

.ລ້ວພະ ເຈົ້າ ໄດ້ຊ້ງຍືນວ່າ..CAPT..J. de Domenico............ໄດ້ບັນ
ສນາຊິກຂອງຄນະກັມະການບະຫວາງຊາດເພື່ອກວດກາ ຄວາມສງບໄນປະ ເທສລາວ ໄນເວລາ
ປະຕິບັດງານນີ້ ເພີ່ນມີສິດພິເສດຢ່າງນື່ງຊື່ງຕິດລິງຈາກກສານໂລກທີ່ຽງ ເຊີແນວ.

ເພີ່ນໄດ້ເຂົ້າ ຮ່ວມກັບຄນະ ທີ່ຕັ້ງຢູ່......SAMNEUA.................

.........ໂດຍມີສິດທອງ ຫ່ວງ ຢ່າງສດອກ ເພື່ອຄອຍຮັບຕ້ອນ ຂອງງວ ຈງ ຊິດ ພິລະ ເຮືອນ ແລະ
ທະຫານ ທີ່ມີກິຈການ ໄປຮ່ວມ ກັບ ຄນະກັມະການກວດ ຄວາມ ສງບເສິກ ບອກຈາກການເດີນສດອກ
ທີ່ບັນຍຸດ ໄວ້ນີ້ແລ້ວ ຢ່າງມີຊື່ງ ຂອງ ຮ່ວມ ຕິວ ແລະ ເອກສານ ຕ່າງໆ ນັ້ນ ກໍຕ້ອງ ກໍກັບ ສິ່ງ ໄຫ້ສດອກ ດ້ວງ ງວ.
ສານ ໂລກທີ່ ເຊີ ແນວ ໄດ້ຕິກລິງ ໄຫ້ທັ່ງ ຂອງ ຢ່ວຍ ເປັນ ຕູ່ອ້າ ນວຍ ໄນການ ຂນ ສິ່ງ ສິ່ງ ຂອງ
ແລະ ເອກສານ ຕ່າງໆ.

Major General

ເລຂາທິການຂອງຄນະກັມະການກວດ

ຄວາມສງບໄນປະ ເທດລາວ

ICSC identification letter in Laotian

INTERNATIONAL COMMISSION FOR SUPERVISION AND CONTROL IN LAOS

Vientiane, the 1 February, 1955,

I hereby affirm that   CAPT. J. de Domenico

is a member of the staff of the International Commission for

Supervision and Control in LAOS. As such he is entitled to all the

immunities and privileges guaranteed by the two Parties under the

GENEVA Agreement.

He is appointed a member of the Fixed Team based at SAMNEUA .

As a member of this Team and in company with the Team he has

the right to move freely and shall receive from the local civil and

military authorities all facilities that the Team may require for the

fulfilment of the task entrusted to it by the International Commission.

These facilities include provision of personnel, access to documents

needed for supervision, summoning of witnesses needed for anquiries,

security and freedom of movement of the inspection teams etc.

The Team shall be provided by the Parties to the GENEVA

Agreement with such modern means of transport, observation and

communication they may require.

SECRETARY-GENERAL
INTERNATIONAL COMMISSION
FOR SUPERVISION AND CONTROL IN LAOS

1 FEB 1955

ICSC identification letter in English

Chapter 4

SAM NEUA

THE SECOND ROTATION of Canadian personnel occurred just a few weeks after my return to Vientiane. I was ordered to join Major David Fromow, Royal Canadian Artillery in the small but important village of Sam Neua It was considered, rightly as it turned out, one of the two "hard" team sites in Laos. I therefore approached my next posting with understandable misgivings. The fact that a *laissez passer* in three languages and signed by General Guyani himself was, for the first time, issued to individual team members seemed rather ominous. I consoled myself by reasoning that perhaps it was just something new and quite routine. Still, they had not been required at Savannakhet or Vientiane.

The flight to Sam Neua (some maps spell it Xam Neua) was by an Aigle Azur light aircraft. It was only a short flight but the landing was adventurous to say the least. The Sam Neua air strip was ringed tightly by mountains. It was very short and it was traversed diagonally by a deep, wide ditch about half way along its length. To effect a landing, it was necessary to skim over the mountains, drop down quickly and then glide down to the strip keeping the power handy in order to leap frog over the ditch. To make matters worse, this tricky manoeuvre had to be repeated. The first task was to buzz the strip in order to scare off the wild ponies and buffalo that grazed on the grass growing on the strip, and then come around once more to actually land. Our pilot was superb. The manoeuvre was old hat to him. It was not so with me. I had to gulp hard to rid my throat of the apple-sized lumps that formed there.

The author in Sam Neua drafting the team's report

The team was lodged in a large villa which had once been the residence of the governor of the province; it had seen better days. The walls were pockmarked with bullet and shrapnel holes. They were badly cracked in places as well but, on the whole, the villa itself was weather-proof. The grounds were overgrown with weeds and there was a small orange orchard at the side. A waist-high stone wall enclosed the grounds and there was a stone gate opening. The wall had been badly damaged by mortar fire. The interior had also suffered damage. Large patches of plaster had fallen down from the ceilings, the floors were cracked and the plumbing was conspicuous by its absence. Numerous rats lived in the ceiling and, as you lay in bed, you could see their tails hanging down from the openings in the ceiling. Our heating system (it got cold this far north) consisted of a large, open fireplace but there was very little wood to burn. There was little by way of furniture. My room was equipped with an old, large, four-poster bed with a mosquito net and some parachutes for a mattress. These proved to be quite comfortable except for a restless sleeper like myself. As one tossed and turned the parachute hardware worked its way into the small of one's back. We ate at a rough six-foot picnic table with a bench along each side. We sat around on broken chairs and scrounged ammunition boxes. The villa was by no means comfortable but it was adequate for our needs. Indian army cooks prepared our meals and we were each assigned a Laotian boy who attended to such personal needs as laundry.

Sam Neua is located in northeast Laos almost on the border with North Viet Nam. In the days of French rule, it was the seat of the governor of the province of Sam Neua. The village consisted of a cluster of huts and small houses built on both sides of the only village street. The jungle crowds in on the village which is the transportation hub for a number of tracks and dirt roads leading in many directions. Route Colonial 6, the most important of these, links Hanoi to Laos. It had fallen into a state of disrepair and, in many spots, it had succumbed to the persistence of the jungle. The road must have seen a great deal of traffic in war because it was used as a supply route by the Vietnamese guerrillas operating in Laos. It was selected as a team site because the Commission wanted a vantage point from which to observe the progress of the armistice. With Phong Saly in the northwest watching the routes leading into Laos from China, Sam Neua was the Commission's right eye. Sam Neua was also the site of one of the headquarters of the Pathet Lao although we were never able to determine its precise location or its importance in the Pathet Lao's chain of command.

The Pathet Lao, or Lao People's Liberation Army, was the military arm of the Lao Patriotic Front (Neo Lao Hak Sat or NLHS). This army was formed in Viet Minh held territory. They entered Laos in 1953 and seized control of the provinces of Phong Saly and Sam Neua.

The Pathet Lao soldiers were mostly very young men, boys almost. They had been led to believe that they were liberating their country not only from the French but also from the royalist regime in Vientiane. The Pathet Lao conscripted their soldiers at the age of thirteen. They were slightly built and were dressed in brown coveralls, a baseball cap of the same colour with an embroidered red star was worn jauntily on the back of their heads. Their footwear consisted of a rubber sole made out of old vehicle tires and held on to their feet by leather straps.. They were armed to the teeth although they did not seem very warlike to us. They were a very friendly lot most of the time, always smiling and always ready to please their new guests. The soldiers often dozed at their posts with their rifles cradled between their legs. They loved to dance Laotian dances forming a circle, singing and clapping their hands to a languid rhythm. Unlike most soldiers, they did not seem to take a great deal of interest in the local girls who were admittedly non-descript and shabby looking.

The Pathet Lao local commander provided us with a number of these soldiers who doubled as house-boys and gate guards. They seemed to have instructions not to let Canadians out of their sight because, whenever we went for a walk, one of the two gate guards would sling his rifle over his shoulder and trot behind us at a discreet distance. We used to amuse ourselves by walking out in pairs and walking to a fork in the track. One of us would take one prong while the other proceeded along the other. Our body guard used to get very upset about this and would call nervously back to his back-up at the gate of our villa. We thought it best not to go too far away in case the guard's sense of humour wore too thin. After a hundred yards or so, we would turn around and come back to the fork in the track where the guard greeted us with relief written over his face, smiled and followed us back to the villa. They soon caught up to our tricks and, after a while, there were always as many guards as there were strolling Canadians.

On the parachute bed in Sam Neua

Our improvised kitchen in Sam Neua

The author has a
quiet read in his room
in Sam Neua

We protested at being followed wherever we went because, under the terms of the Geneva agreement, we were supposed to have freedom of movement. They did not dispute this right but countered with their responsibility for our personal safety. They pointed out that numerous tigers had been sighted nearby. We had not seen or heard any tigers and felt like saying that with what seemed to be their standard of marksmanship, our guards would not have been able to provide much protection from carnivores.

Actually, there were tigers in the area. Early one morning, we were awakened by the sound of light machine-gun fire coming from the village. We dressed hurriedly and went to investigate. A tiger cub had been cornered by a number of soldiers who were pouring automatic fire into the poor little thing. There was not too much left of the cub by the time they had finished with it. Wisely, the mother did not come to her cub's rescue. On another occasion, a group of young soldiers paraded a dead tiger with its front and rear legs tied to a bamboo pole through the village. I was anxious to buy the beautiful skin but, apparently, it had already been spoken for by someone higher in rank than me.

The Sam Neua area had seen a great deal of fighting. On one of our walks, we located a French cemetery where several French soldiers were buried. The head stones were inscribed with Italian, German and English names and informed the observer that they were

Guard of Honour for Indian Ambassador

The author's personal
attendant

Open air haircut in
Sam Neua

Two of "the boys"

soldiers of the French Foreign Legion. The cemetery was in a scandalous state of disrepair. The graves were overgrown with weeds and many of the head-stones were broken and lying on their sides. We protested this. The answer, with a shrug, was:"they are dead, aren't they?"

Occasionally, we were invited to a village dance. Men and women formed a circle on a buffalo pasture complete with large, fresh droppings. It is no wonder that we stepped gingerly and looked awkward; they were always laughing at us. The men and women would dance around the circle, singing one of their catchy folk songs and clapping their hands. It was strictly a no-touching proposition and there was much weaving of hands in swan-like gestures. These were happy occasions and it was fun seeing these young men having a good time and laughing at us.

We also made our own fun. We were not able to get any liquor supplies except a small ration of cognac which, sensibly, the French included in the combat rations for their troops and which were dropped to us by parachute. We managed to concoct a drink we dubbed "shellac" because of its yellowish-brown colour. The ingredients were canned milk, orange freshie, and the cognac ration. It was warmed in a mess tin over the fire in the hearth and really tasted quite good. I know it was a very good sleeping potion. One evening we overdid the shellac a bit. I woke early the next morning and smelled a beautiful aroma. It came from the orange grove in the villa's garden and the trees were in full blossom. When I wrote to my wife to describe the aroma, I told her that I thought that I had died and I was in heaven. "What" she tartly replied "made you think you were ever going to go to heaven?"

An unforgettable, daily event in our lives was watching the boys kill a number of chickens for dinner which, incidentally, was always curried chicken. A flock of chickens were penned in the courtyard. The boys would herd a few into a corner of the courtyard and then, amidst much merriment would proceed to almost stone them to death. They would then pull a wing feather out of each dazed chicken and drive it through the bird's brain. It was not a pretty sight and it is no wonder that our chickens were always so tough. They got a lot of exercise by the time their turn came for the pot.

We also had some monkeys in the courtyard. They were always begging for food. We were visited by Mr. Norman de Poe, the CBC roving reporter. He became quite attached to these monkeys and

Pathet Lao soldiers dancing with their girlfriends

would feed them scraps from the table. We begged him to cease and desist but he continued this practice until, one day, one of the monkeys climbed up to Norman's shoulder and urinated down his shirt. That, I believe, was the end of the free meals for the monkeys!

Out of the blue, an American aircraft flew over Sam Neua and released a number of parachutes. To our astonishment, some of the parachute skids contained large quantities of packets of butter. The Laotians are not partial to dairy foods and used the butter to pomade their hair. In no time at all also, packets of butter started appearing on the empty shelves of Sam Neua's grocery store. The Chinese owner sold the butter for exorbitant prices or shipped it to Saigon where the

Air dropping of rations and mail for the Sam Neua team

The Otter was wrecked when a wild pony crossed the strip at
the wrong time

market was more favourable. Some other parachutes were loaded with
cases upon cases of canned beer. Unfortunately, some of these
parachutes did not open and the beer came crashing down on to the
village main street. Many of the cans were smashed open and there
was beer spurting all over the place. Fortunately, none of the villagers
was hit. Once again, Laotians did not seem partial to beer and the cans
that survived the air drop soon ended up on the black market.

At about this time also, my beautiful white shark skin suit came
to a grievous end. I was strolling along the river and came upon my
boy who was doing my laundry. He had washed the suit in the muddy
waters of the river and was now in the process of wringing the water
out of it by beating it against a tree trunk. There wasn't much left of
the suit by the time I persuaded him to stop.

Life in Sam Neua was not all beer and skittles. We carried out a
number of reconnaissances when we were able to persuade The
Pathet Lao to allow us to do so. These entailed driving our jeeps as far

as the end of the track and then carrying out a long route march through paths in the jungle. Of course, we never did see anything because we had to give ample notice of our intentions leaving the Pathet Lao command plenty of time in which to disguise anything that was occurring in the areas which we intended to visit. We were of course intent on observing any troop movements or the flow of military supplies into the Sam Neua area.

Within a week or so of my arrival in Sam Neua we received reports of a battle that was taking place to the northeast. It seemed that some royalist troops, secretly supplied by French airdrops, were still manning some high ground which, according to the Geneva agreement, they were supposed to have evacuated many months ago. According to our reports, the Pathet Lao had decided to use force to clear this pocket out. We hastily mounted our jeeps and bumped our way some twenty kilometres over a very rough jungle track. The sound of small arms and mortar fire became quite pronounced as we approached the battle area. Before we knew what was happening, we found ourselves right in the middle of things. There was indeed a small battle going on and small arms fire was being directed both ways. We decided we would first of all try to stop the firing. There was not much we could do but walk right into the middle of the fire zones frantically waving our white flags with ICSC letters. Though highly dangerous, it succeeded and the fire died down. The Pathet Lao attackers drifted into the jungle and we climbed to the mountain strong-point. It was a bald, inhospitable hill-top. Dug-outs and fire trenches had been in use by the defenders and there was plenty of evidence of mortar craters. The strong-point was manned by a motley group of mountain folk, labelled Montagnards, commanded by two young French officers. We got conflicting reports about who had started the fighting and we got into arguments with the Poles trying to establish the likely trajectories of the weapons used. It was all quite useless of course but it would look good for the Poles if they could persuade us that, in spite of the illegal presence of the French-led Montagnards, it was they who had initiated the fight. The evidence, in our eyes, pointed to the certainty of an attack by the Pathet Lao. Since the presence of this small unit was undoubtedly illegal, there were other means, we pointed out, of resolving the matter. The Pathet Lao, for example, could easily have asked us to intervene before force was resorted to. The report we submitted held the usual minority view. In the final analysis however, we had stopped the fighting and, making sure that the French commander understood that his unit must evacuate the strong-point, we made our way back in the fast-approaching darkness. We did not see any casualties among the Montagnards and we would not have known if there had been any among the Pathet Lao. We never knew whether the French-led unit ever did evacuate the strong point. Presumably, the Commission brought the matter up in their deliberations and that appropriate action had been taken. During the remainder of my tour of duty in Sam Neua, we never heard anything more about it and reports of fighting ceased. We let matters stand there.

My last few days in Sam Neua were very dark. In one week, we received two mail airdrops. In one letter from my brother in Malta, I read about my mother's death. The other letter contained the news that, soon after, my father had died. I considered the possibility of asking for some leave to attend the funerals but dismissed the idea. It was too far away and I would never make it in time. It would have been very expensive and we were getting short-staffed in Laos. There had been some who had been evacuated back to Canada for various reasons.

My parents had been married for over fifty years and had had sixteen children, many of whom lived in different parts of the world. My father undoubtedly died of a broken heart. It was all very sad. To make matters worse, I fell victim to a severe attack of tonsillitis. My throat seemed to be on fire, I ran a rather high fever and shivered in the heat of the day. There was no doctor within two hundred miles and there was no question of a tonsillectomy even if I could have been evacuated to Vientiane as our Canadian doctor—probably quite rightly—distrusted the Vientiane hospital. The only remaining alternative was to evacuate me back to Canada. I badly wanted to finish my Indochina tour of duty. Armed with every pill in our first aid box, I managed to stick it out.

Dear old Rea came out to visit us and we tried to make him as comfortable as possible. I even gave up my parachute mattress and slept on the floor. It was just like Rea to visit the troops in the remotest deployments and we appreciated his sacrifice of basic personal comforts. He expressed a great deal of interest in the degree of freedom of movement we were being allowed. He was disappointed to hear that our situation was no different than that of other team sites which, according to Rea, were experiencing the same difficulties. He told us that this was a hot issue at Commission headquarters and that

Laotian women fishing for snails

the mobile teams were particularly adversely affected. While these were allowed to travel to specific areas where some trouble had been experienced, if they saw anything along the route, they were only allowed to observe and not investigate. They were only to investigate in the specific area they had been authorised to go to. The fixed teams were restricted to a ten-kilometre-wide strip along the fifty-five-hundred-mile long frontier with Viet Nam. Communication routes that were outside the ten-kilometre strip could be used if they were the only available routes giving access to their destinations but again, they could only observe, never investigate. Besides making travel difficult, these restrictions did severe damage to the credibility of the Commission.

Administratively, things were improving for us. A Rest and Recuperation (R&R) policy was put into effect allowing each of us to go on a ten-day leave to either Hong Kong or Singapore after six months' duty in Indochina. A change of scenery was badly needed at the six-month point and we were all very grateful. Payment of a "hard laying" allowance had also been authorised. It was not a substantial sum of money but it helped mitigate the effects of the inflationary

The author with Meo women

pressures to which we were subjected. In Laos, for example, prices were three times as high as they were in Canada for even the very basic needs. A tube of toothpaste, for example, cost three times as much at the official rate of exchange in Laos as it did in Canada. We heard a great deal of rumours concerning the black market in currency. We were allowed to draw a portion of our pay in American dollars and these could be traded to local currency at very favourable rates. The centre for these activities was in the bigger cities of Indochina and particularly Saigon. Facilities for black market currency trading simply did not exist in Laos; the local businessmen, it seemed, lacked the business acumen and entrepreneurship necessary for these kinds of activities. It was alleged that some quite senior members of the Commission dabbled but these were only rumours as far as I could make out. There were other possibilities for less-than-legal accumulation of wealth. I speculate that it would not have been very difficult to buy opium in Laos and transport it in our luggage to Saigon. Opium was a legal medium of barter in Laos and we could travel through the countries of Indochina without any customs examinations.

Four weeks was about all one could take of places like Sam Neua, interesting and exciting though they may have been. I was relieved when orders came through that I was to catch the first flight out to Vientiane and that my next posting was to be a "semi hard" team site in Xieng Khouang on the Plain des Jarres some hundred miles northeast of Vientiane. First however, I was allowed some R&R and I settled on Hong Kong.

The aircraft that came to pick me up was the same dear old Dragon of Aigle Azur. This time, I had no choice. It was that or wait for the next flight of heaven knows what type of aircraft on some unspecified future date. I loaded up my gear and the pilot prepared for take-off. The pilot gunned the engine as much as he dared, the Dragon lurched forward, gained speed and lifted itself just enough for its fixed under-carriage to clear the brow of the ditch by a whisker. We floated over the top of the mountains and headed for Vientiane.

Chapter 5

HONG KONG

I OPTED FOR HONG KONG because that is what most of my friends had chosen and they all spoke highly of the place. The government paid our return air fares from Saigon but we had to make our own travel arrangements. Food and lodging were the responsibility of the individual.

With a navy friend of mine, Commander Tom Connors, I flew out of Saigon aboard a Dragonair plane. It is funny how we allow stereotypes to bother us. The name Dragonair calls up visions of elderly pilots flying poorly maintained aircraft. The name should not have bothered me; many years later I flew into Sioux Lookout on Bearskin airlines! Anyway the flight to Hong Kong was uneventful and a perfect touchdown was achieved in spite of the nearby mountains.

Many Canadians had preceded me to Hong Kong and a firm link had been established with an enterprising Chinese businessman named Gene Lu. Gene and his very beautiful wife would meet the Canadians at the airport and escort them to their home for tea. They would confirm your hotel reservations for you while displaying several samples of material and a clothing style book. You could choose two or three civilian suits and Gene would measure you up. After tea, he would escort you to your hotel and then, together with his wife, would later pick you up and take you out for a bang-up dinner as their guests at a posh Chinese restaurant. Gene's wife also offered to take us out shopping the next day. She selected the shops that offered good stuff and bargain for you in Chinese for whatever it was that you wanted to send home. The duty-free port of Hong Kong offered numerous bargains in jewellery, electronic gadgets and brocades. I selected a lovely piece of brocade which Madge later made into a beautiful evening gown.

The next morning, the clothes you had ordered were delivered by the hotel porter who hung them neatly in your room. Mine was a perfect fit including the width of the sleeves. The cost of a suit was about thirty-five Canadian dollars. Gene maintained a file with your measurements so that you could continue ordering clothing from him. It was an excellent arrangement and many of us took advantage of it years after our return to Canada. I suppose Gene made a fortune out of it and probably had a sweat shop going all night.

Hong Kong is located on the southeast coast of China. The metropolis is congested and boasts one of the world's largest, natural deepwater harbours where, every year, about twelve thousand ocean-going vessels call in. The scene from the tall mountains that rose from the sea was one of dynamic panoramas and rugged terrain. Victoria, the capital, is on Hong Kong Island. Its streets climb almost vertically half way up Victoria Peak. The major commercial centre is in Kowloon directly across the harbour.

Canadian guests of Gene Loo

John and June Blackstock

Because of the steep terrain, ninety percent of the mostly Chinese population live on fifteen percent of the land area creating the highest population density in the world. It literally teems with people. The climate is very mild and, except for the typhoon season in late summer, very pleasant.

Hong Kong was everything it was cracked up to be. The hotels were modern, clean, comfortable and inexpensive. The city streets were clean and the Gurkha police were smartly turned out and, as far as I could tell, kept the city free of crime and beggars.

The famous Gurkhas are recruited by the British and Indian armies. Through the years, they have come to be regarded as the finest soldiers in the world.

Gurkhas come from the small, landlocked country of Nepal which lies along the southern slopes of the Himalayan mountain range between India and the Tibet autonomous region of China. Three quarters of Nepal is mountainous terrain. It is one of the least developed countries of the world. Except for the city of Katmandu and other smaller centres of population, Nepal consists mainly of villages and small trading centres.

The British and Indian armies highly regard Gurkha units. The men are of small physical stature, take a great deal of pride in their soldierly appearance and respond very well to military discipline. A number of Gurkhas have won Victoria Crosses in past wars. They are a mountain people and have displayed the fighting qualities often

Picnic at St. Andrews Bay

At the floating restaurant

associated with people who are accustomed to living in harsh, mountainous terrain. On their belts, they carry a fearsome, curved knife called a "Kukri." In battle, they favour the silent, night attack and kill their enemies by slitting their throats.

Gurkha units were also used by the British to perform duties of a general security nature. In Hong Kong in 1954-55 for example, the Gurkhas provided general policing although they were ventually replaced by the Royal Hong Kong Constabulary.

Hong Kong's hundreds of shops were well stocked and the prices for their goods were very reasonable. Excellent restaurants abounded featuring different cuisines and five star service. We went to a floating seafood restaurant in the nearby village of Aberdeen. I sat in the very chair occupied recently by the American film star Clark Gable—or so I was told. We chose from the live fish which were swimming around a tank which was lashed to the side of the barge on which the restaurant was built. The fish you selected was cooked and served piping hot complete with head and tail on a silver platter. It was on the spicy side but was absolutely mouth-watering. There were lots of theatres, night clubs, a golf course, a horse racing track and a cricket field. Taxis were plentiful and we enjoyed crossing the harbour to Kowloon in a water taxi or, as they are called, a "wallah-wallah boat".

An old British army friend of mine, Major John Blackstock of the Royal Artillery, happened to command an anti-aircraft battery stationed on Stone Cutters Island, a small island in the middle of the harbour. In 1953, he and I had attended the Long Gunnery Staff Course in Wales. Blackie and his wife June lived in a penthouse apartment in a high-rise at the very top of a mountain called "The Peak." Their balcony was often just above the clouds that drifted over Hong Kong. Standing on that balcony on a cloudy day gave one an eerie feeling. The Peak overlooked the very busy harbour with its colourful Chinese junks, sleek Royal Navy war-ships, cargo and passenger ships of many flags, car ferries and, of course, hundreds of wallah-wallah boats. June and John were very hospitable and made sure Tom and I took in all the sights of Hong Kong. We even had tea among the aspidistras in the lobby of the Peninsula Hotel where a very British-looking string quartet in the lobby entertained the guests. We had an unforgettable picnic on the sandy beach of St. Andrews Bay where we ate the delicacies which June's cook had prepared and carefully packed in June's picnic basket that looked as if it had been bought from Harrod's.

Understandably, Hong Kong was a much sought-after posting for British officers.

Time, of course, absolutely flew by. As I luxuriated in the hotel's hot baths I revelled at the magic of it all and blessed our superiors for the opportunity of this brief respite from the harshness of Indochina. But every city unfortunately has its seamy side. We were saddened to note that thousands lived like ants in the less prosperous area of the city. They lived in shanties built into the side of the mountain or on some of the junks which were permanently moored in the typhoon shelter in the harbour. It is too bad that abject poverty had to exist among such contrasting prosperity.

Speaking of poverty, I was fast running out of money. Noting this, Blackie very kindly invited me to stay the last two days at the officers' quarters on Stone Cutters Island. I was given a spacious room and a batman to look after my needs. Tom was still in a good financial state so he decided to stay on at the hotel. On the day of my departure Blackie and June saw me to the airport; we said our goodbyes and Tom and I boarded the plane for Saigon. It had been a fascinating experience.

We arrived in Saigon in time to catch the Commission aircraft flying to Vientiane and, once again, the Setha Palace Hotel beckoned. The next day, I reported for my flight to Xieng Khouang. This time, I took a chance with Air France.

Chapter 6

XIENG KHOUANG

THE AIRSTRIP OUTSIDE XIENG KHOUANG is ringed with high hills. Whatever the wind direction, a sudden drop in altitude is necessary to reach the beginning of the runway. Like Sam Neua, the airstrip is also a favourite grazing ground for wild pigs, ponies and buffalo which have to be buzzed before a safe landing can be effected. Thus it is necessary to make at least two of these hair-raising manoeuvres before the final touch-down. We finally negotiated our way down and rolled to a stop at the grassy apron. A small crowd of towns-people always turned up to watch the plane landing no doubt hoping to see something spectacular. They gave us a friendly clap when we tumbled out of the aircraft and helped us with the baggage.

The small town of Xieng Khouang (some maps spell it Xiengkhoang) is located on a plateau some four thousand feet above sea level at a distance of about one hundred fifty miles Northeast of Vientiane. It is set in hilly, savannah-type country astride important routes linking the Thailand border at Vientiane with Hanoi and the royal capital at Luang Prabang. Though it is a small town of two or three thousand, it is the administrative capital of the province of Xieng Khouang with a population of about two hundred thousand.

The Xieng Khouang area was the scene of much fierce fighting during the French Indochina war because of its strategic position along the invasion route from the northeast. It is such open terrain that the French must have had a considerable military advantage against a force which was expert at and more inclined to fight a guerrilla war in jungle terrain.

On the plateau to the northwest lies a stretch of flat grass land called the Plain des Jarres. It derives its name from over one hundred stone jars which lie scattered about the area. Some of these jars are over six feet high and they weigh from one to six tonnes. The stone does not come from anywhere near. Experts agree that the jars are about two thousand years old. No archaeologist has yet discovered the purpose that these jars served. Some speculate that they were the drinking vessels of the giant ancestors of the Laotian people. If this is so, then the present day Laotians have shrunk considerably in size. Others theorise that the jars were used as a depository for the ashes of cremated ancestors, giving the area some religious significance. The origin and purpose of these jars remains to this day one of the world's archaeological mysteries.

As far as the Commission was concerned, Xieng Khouang was considered a "semi hard" team site somewhere in between the facilities of Vientiane and the ruggedness of Sam Neua. Xieng Khouang was the northernmost area of Laos which was still under the control of the Royal Laotian government and hence it had something of a frontier town atmosphere.

The "Dragon" light aircraft of Aigle Azur

The stone jars

An old friend of mine, Major Percy Davis, Royal Canadian Artillery, was the senior Canadian team member in Xieng Khouang. He was waiting for me at the airstrip and drove me into the town over the dirt road winding through the Plain des Jarres. On the way, I saw Toby for the first time. His real name was not Toby of course. It was a nickname I gave him. We never did get to know his real name. He was a small, chubby Chinese boy, three or four years old, with dark, limpid eyes. He used to sit on the edge of the kerb, stark naked except for a flimsy T shirt, sucking on a rice ball about the size of a baseball. He sat there and watched the world go by. He later got used to us stopping and handing him a candy. On the odd occasion, we forgot. Remembering, we stopped just past him, walked back and gave him the candy. There was a very large tear rolling from each eye down his chubby, pink cheeks. I have always been amazed at the placid beauty of oriental children. They never seemed to cry.

The team had been allotted a quite respectable bungalow in the middle of the town. At one time, it had been the residence of the governor of the province. It was in good condition and comfortably furnished. Percy and I each had a room to ourselves although, as the junior member, I would be expected to share my quarters with any Canadian visitors to the team site.

I had known Percy for a considerable time and we got on extremely well with each other. He is a tall handsome man with slightly greying wavy hair, a "Rock Hudson"-type face and a trim, well-built frame. His uniform was adorned with campaign medals and he wore the wings of an artillery air observer. The ladies found him irresistible. I often enviously noticed that, without any particular effort on his part, the best looking girls in a room somehow gravitated towards him.

He briefed me on the situation in Xieng Khouang. In spite of the great importance of the area, all was very quiet. There was not much to do except maintain surveillance. Unlike Sam Neua, our hosts were the Royal Laotian Army. The authorities did not obstruct us and had even assigned us our very own helicopter which we parked in our back garden. The French aircrew lived with us and were always anxious to do a bit of flying. Having an airborne taxi at our beck and call made us feel very important.

A number of high ranking Laotians lived in the Xieng Khouang area and a fair amount of socialising was possible. We quickly made friends with the governor of the province and his family and various other local notables and we were sometimes invited to their homes.

Major Pete Petrick
demonstrates the
size of the jars

The team's billet in
Xieng Khouang

The Xieng Khouang schoolhouse

What we then called Dominion Day was fast approaching. Percy and I were anxious to stage some sort of celebration to mark the event and also to repay some of the hospitality we had received. We decided we would invite several people to a cocktail party after which we would use our backyard as an auditorium and show a Canadian movie. We signalled our intentions to headquarters. After some time, they went along with the idea and promised us their one and only film. The film depicted the coronation of Her Majesty Queen Elizabeth II. While this promised to be very colourful and impressive, it was not exactly what we had in mind. We would have preferred a film showing typical Canadian scenes, but beggars cannot be choosers so we went along with the suggestion. The offer to supply the film and the projector was contingent upon us saying that we knew how to operate the equipment and that we would not damage the film in any way. In fact, very stern warnings were given about returning the film promptly and in good condition. I signalled back saying that I was familiar with the Bell & Howell projector which was, to say the least, stretching the truth. The equipment and film arrived the evening of the day before and I did not have time to check it all out. I did notice however that, whereas the film was wound on a thirty-six inch reel, the spare wheels on which the film would wind as it was used up, were only eighteen inches in diameter. I did not give it much thought. I was busy with the last minute preparations and I thought I would later work out some sort of solution to the inevitable problem.

We sent out forty invitations and, in a moment of foolishness, we extended an invitation, just to the movie, to the whole town through the mayor. That, coupled with some afternoon rain which made the ground in our back garden soggy plus the fact that I had forgotten about the discrepancy in wheel diameters, was to be our undoing.

The cocktail party went without a hitch. Percy and I got dressed up in our best uniforms complete with Sam Browne belts. When the rain stopped, it became quite warm. All our guests arrived and the drinks were flowing freely. As dusk approached, the time to show the movie was drawing near. I looked out to the backyard. To my horror,

A foot-powered rice husker

A charcoal heated iron for pressing clothes

it was absolutely jammed with people. All the VIP seats were taken and people were squatting on every square inch of the place. The projector, which I had placed on a rickety table just behind the VIP seats, was barely visible and the extension cable had been trampled several inches into the soft ground.

There was nothing to it but try and proceed as planned. I sent our boys out to chase people away from the VIP seats and to clear a path to them. When the coast was reasonably clear, I nodded to Percy to escort the VIPs out and elbowed my way through the crowd to take up my position beside the projector. It was a hot evening and my dress uniform was no help at all. I was hemmed in on all sides and I could barely reach the projector switch. I was sweating profusely and I was trying to dissuade a little boy from rubbing his runny nose on my sleeve. As soon as the guests were seated, I stretched out and flicked the on/off switch. To my astonishment and relief, power was reaching the projector.

Everyone was oohing and aahing as the coronation scenes unfolded on the wobbly screen. They were much impressed by the pomp and pageantry and everybody was having a good time clapping every time there was a close-up of the Queen. I was feeling proud of myself when I looked down and noticed the film had filled the eighteen inch reel and was spilling onto the muddy ground at my feet. There already were yards of the tangled, wet film. None of the audience was any the wiser it seemed—least of all good old Percy who was having a great time chatting up the governor's daughter. For me, the agony of suspense was endless. I prayed that the movie would end before too many miles of the film were ruined. Finally, the movie ended. Percy escorted the governor's daughter and the rest of the VIPs back to the house. As he passed me there was a twinkle in his eye when he congratulated me on a good job. I could cheerfully have strangled him. Later we had a good laugh over it all. The public relations guy at headquarters was not quite so amused when he opened the box containing the projector and what was left of his film.

Xieng Khouang was a favourite destination for one-day visits from the brass at headquarters. They would fly in by helicopter, spend the day with us and leave in time to catch dinner at their villas in Vientiane. The Indian ambassador came and shook a lot of hands. The local unit of the Laotian army put on a scraggly guard of honour for him which, to my way of thinking, was not anywhere near the standards of the Coldstream Guards at Buckingham Palace. Rea too came to visit but he stayed the night. He was the bearer of excellent tidings for me. I had been selected to attend the Italian Army War College course in Civitavecchia, Italy after my tour in Indochina. Staff College places were not easy to come by and attendance was a prerequisite to more senior positions. While I had hoped to go to the Canadian Army Staff College, I thought that Rome was not going to be too hard to take. I couldn't wait to tell Madge who promptly started trying to learn some Italian phrases. She actually did quite well and by the time we set up house in Italy, she and the maid could make each other understood reasonably well. The plan was for me to return to Canada at the end of my tour in Indochina, pack up the house and move the family. We were to sail on the TN Andrea Doria which later was to come to grief in a collision at sea with a Swedish vessel. The Andrea Doria was the pride of the Italian passenger liners and it would sail from New York to Naples with a stop in Gibraltar. It was very exciting news. Rea had a great deal of fun giving me all the details.

We briefed Rea on all we had been doing, the situation in our area, our relations with the other members of the team and with the local community leaders. We arranged to have him meet some of the community leaders the next day. Rea was much impressed by the fact that a "king" lived in Xieng Khouang. Actually, it was not a king at all. Touby Lyfong, the son of the richest man in the province, was known as the Chao Muong or Paramount Chief. Some interpreter had told Rea that "Chao Muong" meant king. We knew Touby quite well. He was a short, fat fellow dressed in a white suit, white shirt and black tie. He looked like a Mafia don and strolled around in a wide-brimmed panama hat. He sported a thin moustache over his thick lips and, when he smiled—which he often did—you could see that several of his teeth were capped in gold. We estimated that he might be the local exporter of opium but we never knew for sure. Rea had a great time talking to "King Touby" whom he kept on addressing as "Your Majesty." Touby, of course, loved it.

We told Rea about an incident in which the Pathet Lao claimed that the "bandits," as they called the French, had killed a local school teacher. We asked that they exhume the body as proof that someone had been killed. They would only do the exhumation after payment of a buffalo in order to appease the gods. We said we could not do that and the matter was left there. Rea was very amused by the incident.

Rea enjoyed most of his visit with us. I say most because, the afternoon before he was to return to Vientiane, he insisted on doing another reconnaissance. As luck would have it, our jeep drove up a very narrow path which was hemmed in by thick jungle. As we rounded a corner, we came up behind a cart pulled by a slow plodding buffalo. The cart contained six "honey buckets" as we called them and was travelling very slowly. The honey buckets were containers of human waste which the local farmers used to fertilise their fields. The stench was indescribable. We could not overtake the cart nor could we turn around and head away from it. It was a very lengthy journey indeed.

Rea was interested in the flora and fauna of Laos. He even published a pamphlet on the subject. His attention was caught by a hibiscus-type plant which grew quite profusely around our villa. He wanted us to gather up an armful for him to take back and examine at his leisure. By the time we got back from our reconnaissance however, all the blooms had disappeared. We explained that the Laotians considered the plant a delicacy which was very good for the digestion. As soon as a bloom appeared, it was snatched off and put in somebody's salad bowl. Rea's curiosity was also quite piqued by the large rats which scurried around the villa. There seemed to be large numbers of them and Percy and I used to observe their habits. They were always looking for food and mating. They did this continually.

Percy was quite convinced that the Laotians ate these rodents. He refused to eat anything until he had personally inspected the kitchen for rat carcasses. Rea left us the next day and we missed him.

While all was militarily quiet in our area, there always was a stressful feeling about the place. I had the feeling that there was something going on but I could not put my finger on it. We were constantly on the move by helicopter, jeep and on foot. We never did see anything untoward and our reports to Vientiane must have sounded very bland.

My time in Xieng Khouang was rapidly coming to a close and my thoughts centred on the family and particularly our new son Mark whom I had not yet seen. I had one more tour to do before returning home. Our headquarters in Vientiane was busy drafting new Repatriation instructions and I understand that several people had volunteered for another Indochina tour. I am not sure how many were allowed to stay. I think the Canadian Forces did not think too highly about keeping anyone in Indochina longer than one year.

Shortly after Rea's return to Vientiane, both Percy and I were informed that our last Indochina tour would be to the Mobile Team operating out of Saigon (now known as Ho Chi Minh City). Saigon promised to be a very pleasant end to our tour of duty. The Dragon picked us up and we were soon safely back at the Setha Palace hotel. Nothing much had changed at the hotel. The pump attendant grinned happily when he saw us no doubt thinking about all those tips he would get when he re-started the pump. We thought it fitting for us to out-smart him this time. I would stand guard on the pump while Percy had his shower. He would then do the same thing for me. Actually, we also tipped the attendant.

Before leaving Laos, presumably for good, some final descriptions of the customs, life style and religion of the Laotians may be appropriate.

Laotians are great story tellers. A legend they recount concerns a banyan tree, a man, a woman and a lion. It seems that God planted a banyan tree on earth. It grew so big and shaded the ground so much that all the vegetation started to die. God looked at the tree and called for volunteers to cut it down so that the sun could once again reach the earth. Many people came forth but they were not able to work fast enough to cut all of the tree down before it dropped its vines and started growing elsewhere. Eventually, a man and his wife worked so diligently that they succeeded in out-pacing the tree. As they were

The boat races

The man, the woman and the lion

about to deliver the final cut with the axe, the tree fell on them and they were both killed. But God looked after them in the after-life by providing them with a lion to protect them.

Small sculptures of the man, the woman and the lion are to be found outside some Buddhist temples. Larger ones with faces about thirty inches across are used in certain celebrations. Except for certain anniversaries, the large sculptures are kept inside the temple.

I cannot imagine what the moral of this story is. Perhaps it illustrates that God can show gratitude or that even he makes mistakes just as we ordinary mortals do.

Most Laotians practise Buddhism. They participate in all the festivities prescribed by their religion although they did not strike me as particularly ardent Buddhists. You do not see them flocking to their temples. As in most other things, Laotians seem nonchalant about religion.

Buddhism is divided into a number of schools. In Japan and China for example, the "Mahayana" school predominates. In Thailand, Sri Lanka and Laos the precepts of the "Theravada" school are followed. This school believes in the emancipation of the individual through his own efforts.

The basic tenets of Buddhism are observed by Laotians and are reflected in what appears to be their character. They are an easy-going

The stone and mud hut used for meditation

Bonzes with their furled umbrellas

people who seem to be content with their lives. They appear to have come a long way towards achieving "Nirvana," the highest bliss, Buddha's escape from the cycle of rebirth. Laotians are a very gentle self-effacing people. One can imagine them emulating Buddha when he allegedly offered his own body for food to a starving tigress and her cubs.

Buddhist monks, or Bonzes as they are called, roam the streets in most of Laos though they were noticeably absent from Communist controlled centres of population such as Sam Neua. They are most numerous in Vientiane. They stroll the streets in their cotton, saffron-coloured robes, shaven heads and sandals. The young ones carry empty rice bowls cupped in their hands seemingly begging for food. They are friendly looking and salute you with the typical gesture of holding their hands as if in prayer; it is difficult to strike up a conversation with them because they avert their eyes when they are approached.

Small huts made out of stone and mud and with a crawl-size entrance were dotted about the city. They were used by individual Bonzes when they felt the urge to divorce themselves from the world and meditate. Major Pete Petrick unkindly suggests that all they do in these huts is contemplate their navels.

Laotians also have their own brand of fun. An annual boat race is held on the Mekong River. Each boat is manned by groups of up to sixty paddlers representing various villages and organizations. The boats or dugouts start about a mile upriver from where the spectators watch intently. A starter gets the boats on their way and they paddle furiously keeping well apart until they reach a buoy moored in the middle of the river opposite the grand stand. At that point, no holds are barred. Using their paddles and a ramming technique, they attempt to overturn the other boats. When the last boat afloat crosses the finish line it is considered to be the winner.

And now, on to Saigon.

Chapter 7

SAIGON AND HOME

THE FRENCH CALLED SAIGON "The Paris of the Orient." High praise indeed from a Frenchman who holds Paris in such high regard. Saigon undoubtedly earned this kind of reputation in the old colonial days. By the time I reached it in 1954 it was beginning to get a little ragged around the edges. During the heyday of the occupation of the city by American forces, I am told, it reached new levels of seediness. After its capture by North Vietnamese forces in April 1975, it was renamed Ho Chi Minh City and soon probably became much more austere. The Communists have a way of dampening things down as they plainly showed after their take-over of Hanoi in October 1954.

Saigon is the largest city of Viet Nam with a population of about three million. It is now judged to be the most densely populated city in the world because of the many thousands of peasants who were displaced by the war and who sought a better life than the one they experienced in their villages. The shanty towns which had grown around Saigon were not very pretty and, in 1954-55, the sight of large numbers of destitute people sheltering in the once proud Saigon opera house was very haunting. The city was full of beggars. They represented a most un-Vietnamese way of life because, traditionally, the village elders were always taken care of by those who could still earn a living. Pick-pockets, pimps, prostitutes and all sorts of other unsavoury characters rubbed shoulders with shoppers and business people in the crowded streets of Saigon. It was said that Saigon prostitutes earned more in a year than a Vietnamese university professor.

The well paved, broad, tree-lined avenues of Saigon and especially its meaner streets were a nightmare of traffic jams, loud horns and thousands of Japanese cars choked the air with fumes. At one point, Saigon acquired the nick-name "Honda City." Motorcycles with as many as three passengers screeched through the streets. The motorcycle had been transformed by the ingenious Vietnamese into a two-passenger taxi called a "moto-cyclo." The two passengers rode in a sort of upholstered love seat mounted on the motor cycle's two-wheeled front axle. The driver rode in the normal motor-cycle seat at the rear. A ride in one of these moto-cyclos was a hair raising experience since the vehicle was driven at break-neck speed through crowded streets and the passengers would be the first to feel the impact of any crash. There were of course no helmets or seat belts. The moto-cyclo however was a cheap, fast method of transportation and riding in one was something of a dare-devil experience.

Saigon is located in the deltaic plain of the Mekong River in dead flat country covering some thirty-eight thousand square kilometres. It was captured by the French in 1859 and made into the administrative capital of all of French Indochina. In 1954, it became the capital of the Republic of South Viet Nam. It is Indochina's chief sea port some eighty kilometres from the South China Sea. Saigon has a hot and humid monsoonal climate with an average temperature of twenty-six degrees Celsius and an annual rainfall, which occurs between June and September, of seventy-eight inches.

Saigon's Roman Catholic cathedral is an impressive building constructed in 1883. There are also two Buddhist pagodas, a large opera house, a university, public gardens, cinemas and open-air theatres. It is a major fishing, manufacturing and distribution centre. Tan Son Nhut international airport serves both international as well as domestic flights.

Saigon has a number of suburbs of which Cholon is probably the best known. Most of the industries are located there. It is a walled city constructed in 1778 by soldiers and officials who remained loyal to the Ming Dynasty of China. It is far less modern than Saigon proper and has an air of intrigue about it. We were told that Cholon was the headquarters of the Binh Xuyen Secret Society which was reputed to control the Saigon under-world. Numerous houses catered to the Chinese penchant for gambling. A number of Chinese theatres staged highly stylised plays performed to much clashing of cymbals. A fortress-like building in Cholon, called the Palais des Glaces, was reputed to be one of the world's largest brothels. Foreign Legionnaires guarded the entrance gates and enforced a curfew after ten pm. At that hour, the gates were locked. The customer who failed to leave before that time had the choice between spending the night there or scaling the thirty-foot-high walls.

The Binh Xuyen sect, ostensibly a Buddhist organisation, was the official opposition to the South Viet Nam government of President Diem. Several small-scale battles were waged between the sect and government forces. No doubt political control and dominance of the black-market and other criminal activities were at stake. This internal turmoil added to the general instability of the government faced by the military threat for control of the delta posed by the communist forces of North Viet Nam. I had the misfortune of getting caught in one of these battles. We had decided to visit the Fixed Team in nearby Cap St Jacques. This seaside resort was somewhat in the style of the French riviera. It was probably the cushiest posting the Commission could offer in all of Indochina. Our purpose was to establish contact with the team assigned to Cap St Jacques and to familiarise ourselves with the area in the event that we, as a Mobile Team, might have to pay it an official visit to investigate some specific incident. We were on our way back in the early evening in our jeep. There was only one road connecting Cap St Jacques to Saigon. We were about half way home when all hell seemed to break loose. Machine-gun fire opened up from both our front and rear and tracer bullets were arching over our heads, getting closer all the time. We prudently dismounted and took shelter in the ditch and waited for things to cool down. It was all very disconcerting because we could not see who was firing at whom. We could just as easily have been the targets although I suspect it was a scrap between opposing sects. Early in the morning, the firing stopped and the opposing forces appeared to have been withdrawn. We estimated the battle was of about battalion strength because there was a great deal of small arms fire. We were soon able to resume our journey in a degree of safety.

Percy and I were members of a Mobile Team stationed in Saigon. We did not have any specific duties other than to be available should the Commission want some specific thing that needed investigating. The Saigon Fixed Team was primarily concerned with checking merchant vessels entering or sailing from the port of Saigon and carrying warlike supplies. The Geneva agreement sought to control the movement of troops and weapons from or into Indochina, and the Commission had deployed a Fixed Team in Saigon for this purpose. It was a somewhat complicated job and required special expertise as some four million tons of shipping used the Port of Saigon each year. Accordingly, the Fixed Team consisted of naval officers from the three member countries.

Saigon represented the most comfortable of our postings. Our billets were rooms in the four or five star Intercontinental Hotel, a well-run establishment with excellent facilities. We each had a private room with private bath and we were able to indulge in the luxury of a hot bath before dressing for a six-course dinner with wine in the hotel's posh dining room. There was good shopping in Saigon particularly if you had American dollars. I bought Madge a green sapphire dinner ring. I also bought a small stuffed toy in the shape of an elephant for Mark. It was to be my first present for him.

We led quite a leisurely life in Saigon. Although we checked in with headquarters regularly, we were never assigned any tasks. We spent a great deal of our time sitting in the hotel's outdoor café sipping "Pernaud a l'eau," a rather pleasant inexpensive drink which tasted of liquorice, and watching people as they walked by. As homesick soldiers are wont to do, we much admired the very beautiful Vietnamese girls as they strolled by in their native costumes. These consisted of a very tight-fitting, ankle-length silk dress with an up-turned collar and a revealing slit on both sides from the waist down. There were occasions when we had to keep a sharp eye out for pick-pockets who roamed the streets and foreigners seemed to be very special targets. Since I never had much by way of personal valuables or a great deal of money, I was not overly worried.

I do not know why Percy had been selected for the first flight home. I know I was chosen for this preferential treatment because my course at the Italian Army War College was due to start in September and here we were in late July. My wife and I had a great deal to do when I returned home. Our furniture had to be stored, banking arrangements had to be made and all sorts of other things attended to before we could leave for a year's tour of duty *en-famille,* abroad. We thought ourselves extremely lucky to get the posting to Italy. Not only was it going to be a help in my career but Italy was a lovely place where we would meet some very nice people.

When the day arrived for our departure from Saigon, Percy and I said our farewells to the other Canadians in Saigon and headed for Tan Son Nhut airport where the good old Northstar was waiting. We were to retrace our steps and return to Canada via Calcutta in India, Karachi in Pakistan, Basra in Iraq, Cyprus, Malta, the Azores and, finally, Montreal. We enjoyed another two-day stop-over in Cyprus sun bathing, resting and taking in the sights. In Malta I visited the family grave-site and then attended a party organized in my honour by my relatives. I come from a very large family; we were sixteen brothers and sisters in all. The gathering included most of these, their spouses, their children and their spouses and their grandchildren. There were upwards of sixty people there. They wanted to know the details of my posting to Indochina but of course there was too much noise and not enough time. It was a very happy event and I felt somewhat lionized. Of course, my parents were dead and buried and we all missed them very much. I remembered how the "Lizard" had dismissed my request a year earlier for a five-day stop-over in Malta so that I could visit my parents. But it was all spilt milk now. This time, Percy and I were determined to play it cool on the way home and to take advantage of the stop-overs to rest instead of going out on the town and then struggling aboard the aircraft early the next morning. There was not much we could do about the metal bolts sticking out of the centre of the seats but the aircraft was much less crowded and we had room to move around. We also got our share of snoozes in the stretchers which were intended to act as baggage racks, and there wasn't any cargo to block the aisle.

We bumped our way along stopping in Gibraltar, the Azores, Goose Bay in Labrador and finally touched safely down in Montreal's Dorval airport. We were a very tired group of passengers.

The engine noise blunted our senses and we were not able to get any real sleep. At Dorval, we received a very cursory medical check, went through some bureaucratic procedures and completed the usual army paper work. It was good to be back on Canadian soil and I looked forward to the very last leg of my journey by train to Belleville, Ontario.

To my surprise there were no de-briefing sessions. I thought that these would come a day or two later but it did not happen. One would have thought that the authorities would want to find out about our experiences, what problems we encountered and perhaps even ask for any suggestions we had to solve such problems. Perhaps they got all these from the more senior people. I certainly was neither de-briefed orally not was I ever asked for a written report.

During the train journey, I got into conversation with a lady who was travelling west with her two kids. She had been assigned an upper berth and she hinted very strongly that she and her family would be so much better off if only they had, like me, a lower berth in the sleeping car. Foolishly I agreed to switch berths with her. Even more foolishly, I neglected to tell the sleeping car attendant about the arrangement. It was two o'clock in the morning by the time the train arrived in Belleville. I was fast asleep. The attendant reached into the lower berth to awaken me. The lady let out a loud scream, no doubt thinking the worst of the attendant. The train was on the verge of rolling away from the platform. Frantic at my failing to appear on the platform, Madge managed to persuade the conductor that I was aboard and that I was supposed to detrain at Belleville. The conductor was very understanding. He actually delayed the train long enough for me to tumble out of my upper, get hastily dressed, gather up my things and stumble out of the train.

What a home-coming! Madge was very understanding and we drove to our house in Picton, Ontario. My eldest son Nicky had persuaded the baby sitter to keep nine-month-old Mark awake for the occasion and there he was in his yellow sleepers grinning sheepishly at me.

And so, Indochina became a memory, a happy one. It was a relief to be home with my small family again and tomorrow beckoned.

REFLECTIONS

I WAS IN MY TWENTIES when I went to Indochina. And at that age who wastes time reflecting?

Many years ago, we jokingly accused our Career Managers in Ottawa of using the dartboard technique to determine who should go where and to what job. It was alleged that somewhere in the basement of the personnel department building, there was a giant dartboard. Each segment was inscribed with the jobs that were expected to become vacant in the next few months. Each dart bore the name of the officer whose job was due to be changed. When the career manager was faced with a quandary about who should go where, he merely reached down for a dart and threw it aimlessly at the dartboard. This, of course, was not true although it sometimes appeared to be so. It made for a good story. Personally, I shall be eternally grateful to the career manager (Major Jack de Hart I think) who hit the Indochina segment with my dart.

To me, Indochina was an exciting adventure, a new experience, an opportunity to meet exotic (to me) people such as the Poles, the Indians, the French, the Vietnamese, the Laotians, the Cambodians and, last but by no means least, my fellow members of the Canadian forces and the diplomatic staff from our Department of External Affairs. Indochina service brought a brief taste of diplomatic life, an expense-paid holiday in Hong Kong, a sojourn in Saigon, the Paris of the Orient, and protracted visits to the towns and villages of Laos and social exchanges in the homes of some of the Laotian people. Not too many people in their twenties have been so privileged. I was glad to make it back home in one piece after my year's tour in Indochina and happy to be back with my family. I did not reflect too much at that time. The course in Italy was uppermost in my mind.

As one grows older however, one tends to take a harder look at the principal events of one's life. Forty-one years after my Indochina adventure, I ask myself the bottom line question: Did we really achieve anything? With the benefit of hindsight and thinking on the devastating American experience in Viet Nam, on the massacres of the Pohl Pot regime in Cambodia and on the many scars of war in what was once Indochina, I answer the question with a great deal of confidence. Yes, we helped stave off all these horrible things. I say this with no reservations.

It is difficult to answer the question I pose with absolute confidence however because I was not privy to the true benefits which flowed from our efforts. We investigated and reported. Rarely, if ever, were we apprised of the results of our efforts. The Commission, after all, was not accountable to us. Sometimes we saw concrete results such as when we were able to bring to a halt the skirmishes between the former enemies in the Sam Neua area, or witnessed the lifting of a land mine, or saw a family re-united in Savannakhet. So, while I can find no hard proof, I have this warm feeling that we did do some good, as much as could have been done in those troubled times.

In assessing the overall effectiveness of the Commission, it is important to bear in mind that its mandate did not include the resolution of the underlying problem of Viet Nam. While the Ho Chi Minh government was indelibly and unalterably committed to the unification of North and South Viet Nam in the communist image, it would have taken considerable force to cut out the communist cancer in the region. The Viet Nam war proved this beyond a shadow of a doubt. The co-convenors of the 1954 Geneva Conference were well aware of this likelihood. They therefore restricted themselves to the creation of an unarmed force which could only bring about a respite in the proceedings. For fourteen years the Commission laboured to keep a lid on developments in Viet Nam in order to give the Western Powers—principally the Americans—time to meet the inevitable final onslaught. The Commission succeeded in doing this.

The Commission's mandate was to supervise and control the process of a cessation of hostilities in an orderly and credible manner. This the Commission also achieved. Land mines *were* lifted; prisoners of war and civilian internees *were* exchanged; opposing forces *did* withdraw to their assigned areas; the hardships caused to the civilian population as a result of "forced enlistments" *were* minimized; the French *did* evacuate the region in an honourable way. By virtue of its very presence in the region, the Commission held the parties to the agreement to the promises they made when they acquiesced to the terms of the agreement. It is true of course that the parties involved did display a surprisingly co-operative spirit when executing the terms of the agreement. This level of co-operation was due to many factors. The principal factor however was undoubtedly the presence on the ground of tangible evidence—the Commission—that the world at large was watching attentively.

The tasks which had to be carried out to attain the requisite level of normalcy were high priority tasks. Elections were due to be held in Viet Nam in just two years and the two Viet Nams reunited under a democratically elected government. The Commission could not afford to drag its feet. It had to push hard in order to create a climate of normalcy. This was complicated by the fact that there had not been anything resembling normalcy in Indochina for many years. A state of armed insurrection against the French was the normal state of affairs for many years. Moreover, both Vietnamese governments were not anxious to participate in an election they were not sure they would win. The country's difficult terrain and the poor state of its communications further complicated the problem. Even with the best of intentions, the commanders of the two opposing forces experienced difficulty in abiding by the obligations imposed by the Geneva accord.

If the Commission is to be faulted at all, it was in the area of discouraging more vigorously the importation into North Viet Nam of vast quantities of warlike supplies in the years between the cessation of the French Indochina war and the commencement of the Viet Nam war. During these fourteen years, vast quantities of arms and ammunition must have flowed southwards into North Viet Nam; without this, Ho Chi Minh would not have been able to challenge the Americans so successfully. Had North Viet Nam's reinforcement been scrutinized and protested more forcibly the Viet Nam war might have been delayed by a few more years. While the North Vietnamese maintained their averred intention to completely dominate the region, it was inevitable that hostilities would again resume. Blame for this inevitability, cannot be laid on the doorstep of the Commission. It would have taken a very large, armed force to seal the border between

North Viet Nam and China. The only resource from which to raise such a force would have been the US military and the US Congress was obviously unwilling to even consider such a possibility. They would not have wanted to face a Chinese army and they displayed their lack of interest by refusing to ratify the Geneva accord.

Canada took on the responsibility of membership in the ICSC in spite of the political risks in a cold war climate and the financial burden it imposed. We had nothing to gain and we should pay tribute to the dedication of the Honourable Mr. Lester B.Pearson, our then Minister for Foreign Affairs, for his vision. It is no wonder that he was later to be awarded the Nobel Peace prize. We had nothing tangible to gain and I am proud of the fact that we went ahead and did it. Through us and our successors, Canada showed the people of Indochina that "we cared enough to send the very best" as the Hallmark people put it. I am proud also of the fact that I was judged to be good enough to participate in the venture, albeit in a very minor way. After all, I had only emigrated to Canada some seven years earlier.

In so far as Laos was concerned, we provided the breathing space which the government of the day so desperately needed to regroup its forces in preparation for more difficult times ahead. The difficult times did eventually materialize. The Royal Laotian government forces failed to stem the tide of Communist expansion into their country and today, Laos is under Communist control.

We embarked with very little fanfare. We said goodbye to our families at home. There were no tearful farewells on the tarmac of Trenton airport for the media to glamourize. We travelled thousands of miles with not a thought to the possibility of personal danger. We enjoyed a brief respite in Hanoi while the city was still vibrant and we witnessed it succumbing to the drabness of the Communists. We travelled throughout the length and breadth of Laos and did the things we were asked to do. As we went along, we "wrote the book" as they say because Indochina was brand new to us and no manuals of Standard Operating Procedures had been written.

The media did keep a watchful eye on us but there were no sensational happenings to write about. As far as I know, there were no scandals. We had our share of trouble. Some of my colleagues contracted the dreaded disease of amoebic dysentery. Jack Thurrott died in a road accident. A few survived helicopter crashes. When our year was up, we came quietly home and resumed our lives almost as if nothing had happened.

What a magic web Indochina wove! We stared awe-struck at the new things we saw. Our hearts sadden when we think back to how we missed our families, to the run-down military cemetery in Sam Neua or to the Laotian boy who was gored by a buffalo or Jack Thurrott's coffin on the Dakota. Our spirits lift though when we think back to the happy, smiling faces of the Laotian soldiers, or to the dinner in the tent of the Algerian Tabor regiment.

We were treated well. We were even given a medal. We might have been better briefed prior to leaving Canada. We could have used better uniforms. We might have had better mail arrangements so that we could keep in touch with our families. All in all however, the operation was mounted without a hitch which says a great deal for those in Ottawa who planned it. It was also flawlessly directed by our superiors, military and civilian, on the ground in Indochina. This too says a great deal for the flexibility of our people.

When you contrast all that with the events of more recent times, you wonder. It raises so many questions about the politicising of the Department of National Defence, about the blows to the discipline and morale of our armed forces, about the role that the media should play and, most of all, about the ordinary soldier, sailor or airman who puts flesh on political decisions.

The Indochina experience is now forty-three years old. Some will say that the lessons learned from that experience are out-dated and no longer relevant. To paraphrase the philosopher George Santayana "those who do not remember the mistakes of the past are doomed to repeat them." No truer words were spoken.

There are lessons to be drawn from the Indochina experience. Recent peace-keeping events prove that the mistakes of the past may have been forgotten.

The selection of members of our armed forces for peace-keeping roles is worthy of serious consideration. It is not just a matter of choosing names to fill slots. Even when an organized unit is selected to fulfil an overseas duty, it is important that individual members of that unit are carefully screened. When people are sent abroad to perform a peace-keeping role as individuals as opposed to members of an organized unit, there is even more need for screening because, for much of the time, they will be operating more or less independently. What we should attempt to establish before the event is whether or not the person who is selected is psychologically suited to the new role. There is, I think, a case for psychological testing. To my knowledge, this was not done in the case of the first deployment to Indochina. We were lucky that things turned out well. I leave it to the professionals to determine the methods of assessment. The overall aim of such an assessment is to determine the level of personal discipline and the potential for adaptability to a totally new environment. It will undouibtedly be a lengthy and complicated process but, I venture to suggest, it would be an excellent investment.

The briefing of those selected to perform these types of duties is critical. It should not merely consist of a distillation of recent media reports on the destination country, its people and the life-style which will be encountered. Those selected for peace-keeping duties, especially when they are destined for relatively unknown areas of the world, are entitled to know, in as much detail as possible, what they are likely to see, hear and do. Peace-keeping duties involve a great deal of "slack time." To combat boredom which can lead to all sorts of tempting situations, it is necessary to keep tours of duty short. There is no time to learn, on the ground, about the new environment. Again, the Indochina experience was lacking in this respect. And again, we were lucky that the people involved adapted quickly and were able to get to work almost immediately after their arrival in the new theatre of operations.

I do not suppose we fully appreciated, at the time, that although we were unarmed and although our role did not include a police organization's enforcement powers, we did have considerable clout. Why else would the Communist side take such pains to restrict our movements and to conceal any misdemeanours they may have been comitting? The truth lies in the fact that every nation wants to, has to, belong to the world's community of nations. Ostracization, such as that experienced by South Africa until apartheid policies were reversed, is a fearsome weapon. Our Commission had access to the nations which engineered the cease fire agreement and, through them, to the world at large. An international black eye was the last thing that Ho Chi Minh wanted for his country during the formative stages. If we did achieve anything, it was as a result of the clout which flowed from our very existence in Indochina. Whether by armed force or just observation, international peace-keeping operations can have a marked, salutory effect. This point needs to be made in the briefing of those who are being despatched to peace-keeping duty in some corner of the world. Armed with this prior knowledge, they will be better able to perform their duties.

Logistic support is not a frill. It should not be regarded as an area in which manpower economies can be safely effected. If it takes manpower and effort to organize an effective medical and postal system, for example, then it should be done even if it means displacing a few of the "front-liners" to make room for people who have expertise in logistic support areas. This is a difficult problem to resolve especially where a cap has been placed on the manpower allocation. A reasonable compromise should not be impossible to achieve especially if use is made of the available local resources. Reconnaissance parties despatched in the pre-deployment phase should be on the lookout for these resources and the manner in which they can best be tapped. In Indochina, for example, we declined the French offer for the use of their existing mail facilities in favour of the totally inadequate local resources presumably for political reasons. This decision caused us unnecessary hardship.

When people return home after completion of their tour of duty they should be thoroughly debriefed. Speaking for myself, I was not. It was as if I had returned from a period of detached duty somewhere in Canada. If a proper debriefing is not conducted, how are we to know what the mistakes of the past were? How else can steps be taken to avoid those mistakes in the future?

Before delving into the Bosnia and Somalia situations, a caveat. I know very little about these operations. I can only try to interpret the media reports. I believe I can however offer a suggestion. We did not operate within the framework of an organized unit, and we did not need nor did we have any senior non-commissioned officers to micro-manage the troops. Bosnia and Somalia seem to highlight the fact that there is something lacking in the training of our Senior NCOs. These people, by virtue of their standing in the military hierarchy, constitute a vital link in the chain of command. They are usually much more mature people than the troops who serve under them. They are physically closer than the commissioned ranks to the private soldier. In the final analysis, the Senior NCOs are the people who make the wheels turn. Perhaps the problems stemming from the Bosnia and Somalia experiences would not have occurred if the role of the Senior NCO was more adequately understood. This is not to exculpate the commissioned ranks. It is offered as an area which needs, perhaps, more exploration.

In the case of Somalia, there was clearly a need for psychological testing of individual members of the Canadian Airborne Regiment in the pre-deployment phase. Reviewers of the Somalia affair rightly extol the virtues of the overall accomplishments of the Regiment in Belet Huen. It is undeniably true that that the Regiment achieved a great deal of success in restoring a measure of stability and in achieving humanitarian ends. It is even said that the clan chiefs and elders asked that the Regiment be allowed to stay in Belet Huen. It is equally undeniable however, that a few rotten apples were racist and committed intolerable criminal acts. How much more successful would the Somalia operation have been had these rotten apples been identified and dumped out of the barrel before the Regiment deployed in Somalia?

We have had experience with psychological testing. It was employed in the fifties when the first Surface-to-Surface Missile Battery was activated. It was rightly deemed at that time that, because the Battery was to be armed with nuclear tipped missiles and because of the awesome power of these missiles, its members were to be psychologically tested to ensure that they would "press the button" when ordered to do so.

While the Somalia operation was essentially a Chapter VII endeavour, that is, it had a peace-making role, as opposed to a mere peace-keeping role, it also had an important quasi-diplomatic ingredient. This alone should have alerted the senior authorities to the need for special selective measures to minimize the likelihood of trouble.

Before ending this work, I must again pay tribute to all those who helped me with this project. They have already been mentioned so I will say no more in this regard.

"Boomee" is a word which is frequently used by Laotians. It means a variety of things depending on whether it is said with a frown on the forehead or a smile on the lips or with a shrug of the shoulders. In fact, it means "nothing." It could mean "I don't have it" or "there is nothing there." In a more positive way, it has the same meaning as the Spanish "denada", or the French "de riens" or the English "don't mention it." Before I stepped aboard the plane for my final departure from Vientiane, a Laotian officer friend of mine thanked me for coming to his country. I wish I had the presence of mind to smile and say: "Boomee."

Appendix "A"

The two parties have agreed that
this text shall not be published
until further notice
IC/51 Rev.1
21 July 1954
Original: FRENCH

GENEVA CONFERENCE

INDO-CHINA

Agreement on the Cessation of Hostilities in Laos

Chapter 1

Cease-Fire and Evacuation of Foreign Armed Forces and Foreign Military Personnel

Article 1

The Commanders of the Armed Forces of the parties in Laos shall order and enforce the complete cessation of all hostilities in Laos by all armed forces under their control, including all units and personnel of the ground, naval and air forces.

Article 2

In accordance with the principle of a simultaneous cease-fire throughout Indo-China the cessation of the hostilities shall be simultaneous throughout the territory of Laos in all combat areas and for all forces of the two parties.

In order to prevent any mistake or misunderstanding and to ensure that both the cessation of hostilities and the disengagement and movements of the opposing forces are in fact simultaneous,

(a) Taking into account the time effectively required to transmit the cease-fire order down to the lowest echelons of the combatant forces on both sides, the two parties are agreed that the complete and simultaneous cease-fire throughout the territory of Laos shall become effective at 8 hours (local time) on 6 August. It is agreed that Peking mean time shall be taken as local time.

(b) The Joint Commission for Laos shall draw up a schedule for the other operation resulting from the cessation of hostilities.

Article 3

All operations and movements entailed by the cessation of hostilities and re-grouping must proceed in a safe and orderly fashion.

(a) Within a number of days to be determined on the spot by the Joint Commission in Laos each party shall be responsible for removing and neutralizing mines, booby traps, explosives and other dangerous substance placed by it. In the event of it being impossible to complete the work of removal and neutralization in time, the party concerned shall mark the spot by placing visible signs there.

(b) As regards to the security of troops on the move following the lines of communication in accordance with the schedule previously drawn up by the Joint Armistice Commission in Laos, and the safety of the assembly areas, detailed measures shall be adopted in each case by the Joint Armistice Commission in Laos. In particular, while the forces of one party are withdrawing by a line of communication passing through the territory of the other party (roads or waterways) the forces of the latter party shall provisionally withdraw two kilometres on either side of such line of communication, but in such a manner as to avoid interfering with civilian traffic.

Article 4

The withdrawals and transfers of military forces, supplies and equipment shall be effected in accordance with the following principles:

(a) The withdrawal and transfers of the military forces, supplies and equipment of the two parties shall be completed within a period of 120 days from the time on which the Armistice Agreement enters into force. The two parties undertake to communicate their transfer plans to each other, for information, within 25 days of the entry into force of the present Agreement.

(b) The withdrawal of the Viet-Namese People's Volunteers from Laos to Viet-Nam shall be effected by provinces. The position of these volunteers who were settled in Laos before the hostilities shall form the subject of a special convention.

(c) The routes for the withdrawal of the forces of the French Union and Viet-Namese People's Volunteers in Laos from Laotian territory shall be fixed on the spot by the Joint Commission.

(d) The two parties shall guarantee that the withdrawals and transfers of all forces will be effected in accordance with the purposes of this Agreement, and that they will not permit any hostile action of any kind whatever which might hinder such withdrawals or transfers. The parties shall assist each other as far as possible.

(e) While the withdrawal and transfers of the forces are proceeding, the two parties shall not permit any destruction or sabotage of any public property of the local civilian population.

(f) The Joint Commission of the International Commission shall supervise the implementation of measures to ensure the safety of the forces during withdrawal and transfer.

(g) The Joint Commission in Laos shall determine the detailed procedures for the withdrawals and transfers of the forces in accordance with the above-mentioned principles.

Article 5

During the days immediately preceding the cease-fire each party undertakes not to engage in any large-scale operation between the time when the Agreement on the cessation of hostilities is signed at Geneva and the time when the cease-fire comes into effect.

Chapter II

Prohibition of the Introduction of Fresh Troops, Military Personnel, Armaments and Munitions

Article 6

With effect from the proclamation of the cease-fire the introduction into Laos of any reinforcements of troops or military personnel from outside Laotian territory is prohibited.

Nevertheless, the French High Command may leave a specified number of French military personnel required for the training of the Laotian National Army in the territory of Laos; the strength of such personnel shall not exceed one thousand five hundred (1500) officers and non-commissioned officers.

Article 7

Upon the entry into force of the present Agreement the establishment of new military bases is prohibited throughout the territory of Laos.

Article 8

The High Command of the French forces shall maintain in the territory of Laos the personnel required for the maintenance of two French military establishments, the first at Seno and the second in the Mekong valley, either in the province of Vientiane or downstream from Vientiane. The effectives maintained in these military establishments shall not exceed a total of three thousand five hundred (3500) men.

Article 9

Upon the entry into force of the present Agreement and in accordance with the declaration made at the Geneva Conference by the Royal Government of Laos on 20 July 1954, the introduction into Laos of armaments, munitions and military equipment of all kinds is prohibited, with the exception of a specified quantity of armaments in categories as specified as necessary for the defence of Laos.

Article 10

The new armaments and military personnel permitted to enter Laos in accordance with the terms of Article 9 above shall enter Laos at the following points only: Luang Prabang, Xieng Khouang, Vientiane, Seno, Pakse, Savannakhet and Tchepone.

Chapter III

Disengagement of the Forces - Assembly Areas -

Concentration Areas

Article 11

The disengagement of the armed forces of both sides, including concentration of armed forces, movements to rejoin the provisional assembly areas, allotted to one party and provisional withdrawal movements by the other party, shall be completed within a period not exceeding fifteen (15) days after the cease-fire.

Article 12

The Joint Commission in Laos shall fix the site and boundaries:

 – of the five(5) provisional assembly areas for the reception of the Viet-Namese People's Volunteer Forces;

- of the five (5) provisional assembly areas for the reception of the French forces in Laos;

- of the twelve (12) provisional assembly areas, one to each province, for the reception of the fighting units of "Pathet Lao";

The forces of the Laotian National Army shall remain in situ during the entire duration of the operations of disengagement and transfer of foreign forces and fighting units of "Pathet Lao".

Article 13

The foreign forces shall be transferred outside Laotian territory as follows:

(1) French Forces

The French forces shall be moved out of Laos by road (along routes laid down by the Joint Commission in Laos) and also by air and inland waterway.

(2) Viet-Namese People"s Volunteer Forces

These forces shall be moved out of Laos by land along routes and in accordance with a schedule to be determined by the Joint Commission in Laos in accordance with the principle of simultaneous withdrawal of foreign forces.

Article 14

Pending a political settlement, the fighting units of "Pathet Lao", concentrated in the provisional assembly areas, shall move into the provinces of Phong Saly and Sam Neua and will be demobilized where they are. They shall be free to move between these two provinces in a corridor along the frontier between Laos and Viet-Nam bounded on the south by the line SOP KIN, NA MI, SOP SANG, MUONG SON.

Concentration shall be completed within one hundred and twenty (120) days from the date of entry into force of the present Agreement.

Article 15

Each party undertaken to refrain from any reprisals or discrimination against persons or organizations for their activities during the hostilities and also undertakes to guarantee their democratic freedoms.

Chapter IV

Prisoners of War and Civilian Internees

Article 16

The liberation and repatriation of all prisoners of war and civilian internees detained by each of the two parties at the coming into force of the present Agreement shall be carried out under the following conditions:

(a) All prisoners of war and civilian internees of Laotian and other nationalities captured since the beginning of hostilities in Laos, during military operations or in any other circumstances of war and in any part of the territory of Laos, shall be liberated within a period of thirty (30) days after the date when the cease-fire comes into effect.

(b) The term "civilian internees": is understood to mean all persons who, having in any way contributed to the political and armed strife between the two parties, have been arrested for that reason or kept in detention by either party during the period of hostilities.

(c) All foreign prisoners of war captured by either party shall be surrendered to the appropriate authorities of the other party, who shall give them all possible assistance in proceeding to the destination of their choice.

Chapter V

Miscellaneous

Article 17

The Commanders of the forces of the two parties shall ensure that persons under their respective command who violate any of the provisions of the present Agreement are suitably punished.

Article 18

In cases in which the place of burial is known and the existence of graves has been established, the Commander of the forces of each party shall, within a specified period after the entry into force of the present Agreement, permit the graves service of the other party to enter that part of Laotian territory under his military control for the purpose of finding and removing the bodies of deceased prisoners of war.

The Joint Commission shall fix the procedures by which this task is carried out and the time limits within which it must be completed. The Commander of the forces of each party shall communicate to the other all information in his possession as to the place of burial of military personnel of the other party.

Article 19

The present Agreement shall apply to all the armed forces of either party. The armed forces of each party shall respect the territory under the military control of the other party, and engage in no hostile act against the other party. For the purpose of the present article the word "territory" includes territorial waters and air space.

Article 20

The Commanders of the forces of the two parties shall afford full protection and all possible assistance and co-operation to the Joint Commission and its joint groups and to the International Commission and its inspection teams in the performance of the functions and tasks assigned to them by the present Agreement.

Article 21

The costs involved in the operation of the Joint Commission and its joint groups and of the International Commission and its inspection teams shall be shared equally between the two parties.

Article 22

The signatories of the present Agreement and their successors in their functions shall be responsible for the observance and enforcement of the terms and provisions thereof. The Commanders of the forces of the two parties shall, within their respective commands, take all steps and make all arrangements necessary to ensure full compliance with all the provisions of the present Agreement by all military personnel under their command.

Article 23

The procedure laid down in the present Agreement shall, whenever necessary, be examined by the Commanders of the two parties and, if necessary, defined more specifically by the Joint Commission.

Chapter VI

Joint Commission and International Commission for

Supervision and Control in Laos

Article 24

Responsibility for the execution of the Agreement on the cessation of hostilities shall rest with the parties.

Article 25

An International Commission shall be responsible for control and supervision of the application of the provisions of the Agreement on the cessation of hostilities in Laos. It shall be composed of representatives of the following States: Canada, India and Poland. It shall be presided over by the representative of India. Its headquarters shall be in Vientiane.

Article 26

The International Commission shall set up fixed and mobile teams, composed of an equal number of officers appointed by each of the above-mentioned States.

The fixed teams shall be located at the following points: Pakse, Seno, Tchepone, Vientiane, Xieng Khouang, Phongsaly, Sophao (province of Sam Neua). These points of location may, at a later date, be altered by agreement between the Government of Laos and the International Commission.

The zones of action of the mobile teams shall be the regions bordering the land frontiers of Laos. Within the limits of their zones of action, they shall have the right to move freely and shall receive from the local civil and military authorities all facilities they may require for the fulfilment of their tasks (provision of personnel, access to documents needed for supervision, summoning of witnesses needed for enquiries, security and freedom of movement of the inspection teams etc ....). They shall have at their disposal such modern means of transport, observation and communication as they may require.

Outside the zones of action defined above, the mobile teams may, with the agreement of the Command of the party concerned, move about as required by he tasks assigned to them by the present Agreement.

Article 27

The International Commission shall be responsible for supervising the execution by the parties of the provisions of the present Agreement. For this purpose it shall fulfil the functions of control, observation, inspection and investigation connected with the implementation of the provisions of the Agreement on the cessation of hostilities, and shall in particular;

(a) Control the withdrawal of foreign forces in accordance with the provisions of the Agreement o the cessation of hostilities and see that frontiers are respected.

(b) Control the release of prisoners of war and civilian internees.

(c) Supervise, at ports and airfields and along all the frontiers of Laos, the implementation of the provisions regulating the introduction into Laos of military personnel and war materials.

(d) supervise the implementation of the clauses of the Agreement on he cessation of hostilities relating to rotation of personnel and to supplies for French Union security forces maintained in Laos.

Article 28

A Joint Commission shall be set up to facilitate the implementation of the clauses relating to the withdrawal of foreign forces.

The Joint Commission shall form joint groups, the number of which shall be decided by mutual agreement between the parties.

The Joint Commission shall facilitate the implementation of the clauses of the Agreement on the cessation of hostilities relating to the simultaneous and general cease fire in Laos for all regular and irregular armed forces of the two parties.

It shall assist the parties in the implementation of the said clauses; it shall ensure liaison` between them for the purpose of preparing and carrying out plans for the implementation of the said clauses; it shall endeavour to settle any disputes between the parties arising out of the implementation of these clauses. The joint groups shall follow the forces in their movements and shall be disbanded once the withdrawal plans have been carried out.

Article 29

The Joint Commission and the joint groups shall be composed of an equal number of representative of the Commands of the parties concerned.

Article 30

The International Commission shall, through the medium of the inspection teams mentioned above, and as soon as possible, either on its own initiative, or at the request of the Joint Commission, or of one of the parties, undertake the necessary investigations both documentary and on the ground.

Article 31

The inspection teams shall transmit to the International Commission the results of their supervision, investigations and observations; furthermore they shall draw up such special reports as they may consider necessary or as may be requested from them by the Commission. In the case of a disagreement within the teams, the findings of each member shall be transmitted to the Commission.

Article 32

If an inspection team is unable to settle an incident or considers that there is a violation or threat of a serious violation, the International Commission shall be informed; the latter shall examine the reports and findings of the inspection teams and shall inform the parties of the measures which should be taken for the settlement of the incident, ending of the violation or the threat of violation.

Article 33

When the Joint Commission is unable to reach agreement on the interpretation of a provision or on the appraisal of a fact, the International Commission shall be informed of the disputed question. Its recommendations shall be sent directly to the parties and shall be notified to the Joint Commission.

Article 34

The recommendations of the International Commission shall be adopted by a majority vote, subject to the provisions of article 35. If the votes are equally divided, the chairman's vote shall be decisive.

The International Commission may make recommendations concerning amendments and additions which should be made to the provisions of the Agreement on the cessation of hostilities in Laos, in order to ensure more effective execution of the said Agreement. These recommendations shall be adopted unanimously.

Article 35

On questions concerning violations, or threats of violations, which might lead to a resumption of hostilities and, in particular,

(a) refusal by foreign armed forces to effect the movements provided for in the withdrawal plan,

(b) violation or threat of violation of the country's integrity, by foreign armed forces,

the decisions of the International Commission must be unanimous.

Article 36

If one of the parties refuses to put a recommendation of the International Commission into effect, the parties concerned or the Commission itself shall inform the members of the Geneva conference.

If the International Commission does not reach unanimity in the case provided for in article 35, it shall transmit a majority report and one or more minority reports to the members of the Conference.

The International Commission shall the members of the Conference of all cases in which its work is being hindered.

Article 37

The International Commission shall be set up at the time of the cessation of hostilities in Indo-china in order that it may be able to fulfil the tasks prescribed in article 27.

Article 38

The International Commission for Supervision and Control in Laos shall act in close, co-operation with the International Commissions in Viet-Nam and Cambodia.

The Secretaries General of these three Commissions shall be responsible for co-ordinating their work and for relations between them.

Article 39

The International Commission for Supervision and Control in Laos may, after consultation with the International Commission in Cambodia and Viet-Nam, and having regard to the development of the situation in Cambodia and Viet-Nam, progressively reduce its activities.

Chapter VII

Article 40

All the provisions of the present Agreement, save paragraph (a) of article 2 shall enter into force at 24 hours (Geneva time) on 22 July 1954.

Article 41

Done at Geneva, (Switzerland) on 20 July 1954, at 24 hours in the French language.

For the Commander-in-Chief
of the fighting unit of the "Pathet
Lao" and for the Commander-in-Chief
of the People's Army of Viet-Nam

For the Commander-in-Chief
of the forces of the French Union
in Indo-china

TA-QUANG-BOU

General de Brigade

Vice-Minister of the National Defence
of the Democratic Republic of Viet-Nam

DELTEIL

BIBLIOGRAPHY

The following additional reading may be of interest:

Eayrs George James, Indochina: Roots of Complicity, Toronto, University of Toronto Press, 1983.

Fitzgerald Francis, Fire in the Lake: The Vietnamese and the Americans in Vietnam, Boston, Little Brown, 1972. This book provides a very good history of Vietnam to include its foreign relations, politics and government as well as a history of the Vietnamese conflict 1961-1975.

Gardam John, The Canadian Peacekeeper, Burnstown, Ont., General Store Publishing House, 1992.

Levant Victor, Quiet Complicity: Canadian involvement in the Vietnam War, Toronto, Between the Lines, 1986.

Maclear Michael, The Ten Thousand Day War: Vietnam 1945-1975, New York, St. Martin's Press, 1981. This book covers in some detail both the Indochinese war 1946-1954 as well as the Vietnamese conflict 1961-1975.

Nolan Keith William, Into Laos, Novato California, Presidio Press, 1986.

Pike Douglas Eugene, PAVN; People's Army of Vietnam, Novato, California, Presidio Press, 1986.

About the Author

John was born and educated in Malta. During World War II he joined the British Army and served in Malta and Italy. In 1947, John emigrated to Canada and, soon after, joined the Royal Canadian Artillery. During his service, John was posted to Indochina as a member of Canada's delegation to the International Commission for Supervision and Control of the agreement for the cessation of hostilities in Indochina. While he served principally in Laos, his duties took him to Viet Nam, Cambodia, India and Hong Kong.

Upon retirement from the Canadian Armed Forces in 1971, John joined the Government of Ontario. After three years with the Ontario Place Corporation, John was assigned special duties as Ontario's Liaison Officer to the 1976 Olympic Summer Games. John was also entrusted with senior appointments with the office of the Coordinator of two Royal Visits to Ontario. He retired from government service in 1985.

John has been published in various magazines and newspapers and won first prize in an essay competition sponsored by the Conference of Defence Associations. This is his first experience with writing a book.